Matevž Pustišek, Nataša Živić, Andrej Kos
Blockchain

Also of Interest

Security in Autonomous Driving
Obaid Ur-Rehman, Natasa Zivic, 2020
ISBN 978-3-11-062707-7, e-ISBN (PDF) 978-3-11-062961-3,
e-ISBN (EPUB) 978-3-11-062715-2

Multiple Access Technologies for 5G.
New Approaches and Insight
Jie Zeng, Xin Su, Bin Ren, Lin Liang (Eds.), 2021
ISBN 978-3-11-066581-9, e-ISBN (PDF) 978-3-11-066636-6,
e-ISBN (EPUB) 978-3-11-066597-0

Robotic Process Automation.
Management, Technology, Applications
Christian Czarnecki, Peter Fettke (Eds.), 2021
ISBN 978-3-11-067668-6, e-ISBN (PDF) 978-3-11-067669-3,
e-ISBN (EPUB) 978-3-11-067677-8

Technoscientific Research.
Methodological and Ethical Aspects
Roman Z. Morawski, 2019
ISBN 978-3-11-058390-8, e-ISBN (PDF) 978-3-11-058406-6,
e-ISBN (EPUB) 978-3-11-058412-7

Matevž Pustišek, Nataša Živić, Andrej Kos

Blockchain

Technology and Applications for Industry 4.0,
Smart Energy, and Smart Cities

DE GRUYTER

Authors
Assist. Prof. Dr. Matevž Pustišek
University of Ljubljana
Faculty of Electrical Engineering
Tržaška 25
SI-1000 Ljubljana
Slovenia
matevz.pustisek@fe.uni-lj.si

Dr.-Ing. habil. Nataša Živić
Chair for Data Communications Systems
University of Siegen
Hoelderlinstrasse 3
D-57076 Siegen, Germany
natasa.zivic@uni-siegen.de

Prof. Dr. Andrej Kos
University of Ljubljana
Faculty of Electrical Engineering
Tržaška 25
SI-1000 Ljubljana
Slovenia
andrej.kos@fe.uni-lj.si

ISBN 978-3-11-068112-3
e-ISBN (PDF) 978-3-11-068113-0
e-ISBN (EPUB) 978-3-11-068120-8

Library of Congress Control Number: 2021947448

Bibliographic information published by the Deutsche Nationalbibliothek
The Deutsche Nationalbibliothek lists this publication in the Deutsche Nationalbibliografie;
detailed bibliographic data are available on the Internet at http://dnb.dnb.de.

© 2022 Walter de Gruyter GmbH, Berlin/Boston
Cover image: Jian Fan/iStock/Getty Images Plus
Typesetting: Integra Software Services Pvt. Ltd.
Printing and binding: CPI books GmbH, Leck

www.degruyter.com

Contents

List of acronyms and abbreviations

Acronym	Meaning
ABAC	Attribute-Based Access Control
ABI	Application Binary Interface
AI	Artificial Intelligence
AM	Architecture and Mechanism
AMI	Advanced Metering Infrastructure
ANN	Artificial Neural Network
AR	Augmented Reality
ASIC	Application Specific Integrated Circuit
BaaS	Blockchain-as-a-Service
BC	Blockchain
BFT	Byzantine Fault-Tolerant
BGP	Border Gateway Protocol
BTC	Bitcoin
CPU	Central Processor Unit
CSS	Common Style Sheet
CWE	Common Software Security Weaknesses
DAC	Discretionary Access Control
DAG	Directed Acyclic Graph
DAO	Decentralized Autonomous Organization
DApp	Decentralized Application
DDoS	Distributed Denial of Service
DeFi	Decentralized Finance
DER	Distributed Energy Resources
DID	Decentralized Identifiers
DL	Distributed Ledger
DLT	Distributed Ledger Technology
DoS	Denial of Service
DPoS	Delegated Proof of Stake
DSO	Demand-Side Optimization
EAC	Energy Attribute Certificates
ECO	Ecological
EH/s	Exahash per second
EI	Energy Internet
EIP	Ethereum Improvement Proposal
ENS	Ethereum Name Service
ERC	Ethereum Request for Comments
ESI	Energy Service Interface
ETH	Ether
EVM	Ethereum Virtual Machine
GO	Guarantees of Origin
GPS	Global Positioning System
HHC	Hedera Hashgraph Council
HTML5	Hyper Text Markup Language 5
HTTP	Hyper Text Transfer Protocol
IBAC	Identity-Based Access Control

https://doi.org/10.1515/9783110681130-203

IBC	Inter-blockchain Communication
IBTF	Istanbul Byzantine Fault-tolerant
ID	Identification; Identity
IDE	Integrated Development Environment
IoT	Internet of Things
IP	Internet Protocol
IPC	Inter-process Communication
IPFS	Inter-planetary File System
IMEI	International Mobile Equipment Identity
JS	JavaScript
JSON	JavaScript Object Notation
JSON-RPC	JavaScript Object Notation-Remote Procedure Call
LTC	Litecoin
M2M	Machine to Machine
MAC	Mandatory Access Control
MI	Machine Interface
NB-IoT	Narrow-Band IoT
OM	Objective and Model
P2P	Peer-to-Peer
PAN	Personal-Area Networks
PEV	Plug-in Electric Vehicle
PoA	Proof of Authority
PoC	Proof of Capacity
PoS	Proof of Stake
PoSpace	Proof of Space
PoW	Proof of Work
QoS	Quality of Service
RBAC	Role-Based Access Control
REC	Renewable Energy Certificates
RPC	Remote Procedure Call
RWMC	Random Walk Monte Carlo
SCT	Smart Contract Tunnels
SG	Smart Grid
SHA	Secure Hash Algorithm
SLA	Service-Level Agreement
SSI	Self-Sovereign Identity
SWC	Smart Contract Weakness Classification
TC	Town Crier
TCP	Transmission Control Protocol
TEE	Trusted Execution Environment
TLS	Transport Layer Security
tps	Transactions per Second
UP	Universal Protocol
URL	Uniform Resouce Locator
VIN	Vehicles Identification Number
WAN	Wide-Area Networks
WASM	WebAssembly
WebRTC	Web Real-Time Communication

XMR	Monero
XRP	Ripple
ZEC	Zcash

List of notions

Ledger	A book, a list, or other collection of financial accounts and/or transactions.
51% Attack	A potential attack on a blockchain network, where a single entity or organization is able to control the majority of the hash power, potentially causing a network disruption. In such a scenario, the attacker would have enough mining power to intentionally exclude or modify the ordering of transactions.
6-blocks Confirmation	A period of time (commonly around 60 min) necessary for adding six new blocks behind a solved block that contain some transaction. After this period, the transaction is considered confirmed because creating a new version of the blockchain that will not contain a given transaction becomes too difficult, because too expensive in computing power.
Altcoins	Cryptocurrencies other than Bitcoin.
Artificial Neural Networks	A computing system is based on a collection of connected units or nodes called artificial neurons, which loosely model the neurons in a biological brain.
Bitcoin	The most popular cryptocurrency, running on a blockchain created in January 2009 by an unknown person under the pseudonym Satoshi Nakamoto.
Bitcoin/Digital Wallet	A software program for holding and trading Bitcoins which uses a person's private key (secret number) to access the person's public Bitcoin address (an identifier of 26–35 alphanumeric characters) and transaction signatures that need to be securely stored; the Bitcoin wallet comes in many forms – the four main types are desktop, mobile, web, and hardware.
Blockchain	A distributed ledger consists of a series of transaction blocks where each block (except the first and the last) is linked with the previous and next block by means of cryptography, making that way an unbreakable chain of blocks.
Blockchain Fork	A situation within the community (of nodes/members of a blockchain P2P network) that occurs when in the network exist two or more versions of the blockchain (i.e., different nodes may have different versions of the file which contains blockchain data).
Blockchain Mining	A peer-to-peer computer process aimed to secure and verify transactions of a given cryptocurrency (such as Bitcoin).
Border Gateway Protocol	Protocol for routing of IP packets (routing protocol); it is a standardized exterior gateway protocol designed to exchange routing and reachability information among autonomous systems on the Internet.
Branch Tip	A tip that represents the last individual transaction in a branch tip bundle (see IOTA bundle).

https://doi.org/10.1515/9783110681130-204

Byzantine Fault Tolerant System	A system that is tolerant (i.e., resistant) to Byzantine Generals Problem; in the strict sense, a BFT system is capable of functioning properly as long as the number of corrupted elements is less than or equal to two-thirds of the overall number of elements.
Byzantine Generals Problem	A class of failures where some of the components/elements of a system may be corrupted in the sense that they have the symptoms (appearance, behavior) that prevent other system's components from reaching agreement (i.e., consensus) among themselves.
Car-to-Car Communication	Communication that takes place between vehicles with the aim of sharing information that can be used for traffic control or to warn drivers of dangers.
Consensus mechanism	A mechanism (set of rules and protocols) that ensures that all participants dispose of identical copies of the distributed database files (i.e., of the distributed ledger).
Coordinator (in the context of Tangle)	A mechanism implemented by IOTA Foundation with the aim to protect Tangle against vulnerabilities such double-spending (as the Tangle is not fully developed, i.e., the overall number of nodes and hash power in the IOTA network are relatively low); the Coordinator mechanism assumes the issuance of a milestone transaction every two minutes.
Cryptocurrency	A digital currency in which encryption techniques are used to regulate the generation of units of currency and verify the transfer of funds, operating independently of a central authority, i.e., of a central bank; most of the cryptocurrencies are based on blockchain technology.
Cumulative Weight	A metric used within the Random Walk algorithm for tip selection in the Tangle; the cumulative weight of a transaction in the Tangle is the total number (plus 1) of all transactions which came after, and at the same time, approved that transaction directly or indirectly.
Decentralized Application	A computer application that runs on a decentralized computing system. DApps have been popularized by distributed ledger technologies such as the Ethereum blockchain; Smart contracts are a key part of DApps.
Delay Attack	Attack on the Bitcoin's P2P network that also exploits weaknesses of Border Gateway Protocol (similarly as partition attack); in Delay Attack, the propagation of blocks towards a victim node is effectively slowed down, that is, delayed; the main goal is to keep the victim node uninformed about a new block for almost 20 min, which is achieved through a Man-in-the-Middle attack where attacker modifies messages from victim node to the victim's peer node; as the victim's inquiring messages are wrong (due to modifications performed by an attacker), the victim node is unable to get from the network the freshest solved block (in order to add it on its copy of the blockchain); the victim wastes its computing power and time, instead of using it for solving the next block; consequently, the victim loses its possible earnings.

Denial of Service Attacks	A cyber-attack that makes unavailable a host (computer, machine, network resource) connected to the Internet; typically accomplished by flooding the targeted host with excessive requests with the aim to overload the system and prevent legitimate requests from being fulfilled.
Difficulty	The algorithm implemented within Bitcoin blockchain that regulates the level of difficulty for solving the PoW task (block solving), so that in average, the frequency of block solving is one block in every 10 min (i.e., 2016 solved blocks for 14 days); as a parameter, it is defined as Difficulty = Difficulty_1_target/ Target_value, showing how many times it is more difficult to find a 256-bit long hash below current target value (determined by parameter Target_value) than to find a hash below a 256-bit reference target value (determined by parameter difficulty_1_target) which has 32 leading zeros.
Difficulty Target	Name of a 32-bit field in the block header that contains parameter Target_value represented via 24-bit mantissa and 8-bit exponent; content of this field shown in hexadecimal notation is also known as bits.
Digital Twin	A digital replica of potential and actual physical assets (physical twin), processes, people, places, systems, and devices that can be used for various purposes.
Directed Acyclic Graph	A finite directed graph with no directed cycles.
Distributed Ledger	A consensus of replicated, shared, and synchronized digital data geographically spread across multiple sites, countries, or institutions.
Double Hash (or Hash-hash) Algorithm	Generally, double hashing is a computer programming technique used to resolve hash collisions by using a secondary hash of the key as an offset when a collision occurs; in the Bitcoin blockchain, double-hashing is realized through double use of SHA-256 hashing function, that is, $f(x) = sha256(sha256(x))$.
Double Spending Problem	A potential flaw in a digital cash scheme in which the same single digital token can be spent more than once; it appears if two transactions (one of which is tricky) are sent into the network using the same private key of a fraudulent money sender (a buyer in two different transactions), but sent to different receiving addresses (sellers in two different transactions); as two transactions propagate through the network, one part of the network will accept one transaction and the other part another one.
Ethash	A PoW mining algorithm implemented by the Ethereum network and Ethereum-based cryptocurrencies; like SHA-3, Ethash is a hash function that belongs to the same (Keccak) family of hash functions, but differs from SHA-3; Ethash was developed with a strong focus on protection from Application Specific Integrated Circuits miners, who were primarily mining Bitcoins.

Ether	Native token (cryptocurrency) of the Ethereum blockchain; initially, Ether was not seen as a common digital currency with the main purpose as a means of paying goods and services online, but as an incentive mechanism to power the Ethereum blockchain.
Ethereum Blockchain	A decentralized open-source blockchain that features smart contract functionality (a project started in 2013 and led by Vitalik Buterin). It is the second-largest cryptocurrency platform by market capitalization (behind Bitcoin).
Event (in the context of hashgraph)	A data structure created by a node in the hashgraph P2P network at the moment of receiving gossip/synchronization message from another (sending) node; it contains a payload (information about new transactions and other gossips among nodes learned by sending node from the previously received gossip/sync messages), then the timestamp and two hash values that refer to two previous events called self-parent and other-parent event.
Famous Witness (in the context of hashgraph)	A witness of a round that is elected as the famous for that round, in a virtual voting procedure performed by the witnesses of two (or more) upper rounds; it is the witness that most nodes have learned of fairly soon after it was created.
Fiat currency/Fiat money	A government-issued currency that is not backed by a commodity such as gold.
Genesis/Genesis Event	The very first transaction in the Tangle/IOTA in which was created the whole amount of IOTA tokens.
Gossip Protocol	A procedure or process of computer P2P communication based on the way epidemics spread; used by some distributed systems to ensure that data is spread to all members of a group; in some ad-hoc networks, gossip protocol assumes that members forward received data to their neighbors.
Guaranteed (or Secured) Block	A block in a blockchain, after which were added six or more new blocks, it is considered that blockchain forks cannot exist in the blockchain area before the guaranteed block.
Hash Rate/Power	The number of hash calculations per second a computing device is capable of executing.
Hash Value	A numeric value of a fixed length that uniquely identifies (a portion of) data, derived as the result of a hash function applied on the data; as the Bitcoin blockchain uses a hash-hash algorithm, i.e., the SHA-256 hash function implemented twice on input data (header of a transaction block), a hash value (of the header of the previous block in the blockchain) written in the block header (of an actual block) is 256 bits long.
Hashgraph	A permissioned distributed ledger/platform developed by Leemon Baird (in 2016) and supported by Hedera hashgraph LLC that applies the hashgraph algorithm – a new gossip protocol (logically based on a DAG) that enables a full Byzantine fault-tolerant consensus mechanism; besides native cryptocurrency (the Hedera token), the platform is designed to provide other services such as file storage and smart contracts, i.e., the development of permissionless decentralized applications.

Hedera Hashgraph Council	Governing body aiming at supporting the evolution of a stable and decentralized public ledger infrastructure based on the Hashgraph consensus algorithm.
Hedera Hashgraph LLC	A company that launched the Hashgraph project; provides a public ledger platform for the project's support.
Hidden Tip	A tip that is not yet seen by a node due to the propagating delay in the IOTA network.
Industry 4.0	A term used as a meaning for the fourth industrial revolution; as it is not yet completely defined, it rather denotes a set of emerging technologies and tools with a potential to drastically improve various manufacturing processes; it also refers to the synergy between traditional industrial processes and digitalization, whereby the achieved manufacturing solutions are performed through the intelligent networking of machines and processes in the industry with the help of information and communication technology.
Input Transaction (in a bundle)	An individual transaction (in a bundle) with the Value field that contains a negative value, meaning that the account specified by the field Address is charged with the amount of IOTAs specified in the Value field.
Internet of Things	A system of interrelated computing devices, mechanical and digital machines provided with unique identifiers and the ability to transfer data over a network without requiring human-to-human or human-to-computer interaction.
IOTA Bundle	A set of several consecutive individual transactions that represent one complete transaction in Tangle, whereby each individual transaction in a bundle directly approves the previous individual transaction, and all together directly approve the same trunk tip – the last individual transaction in another (previous) bundle called trunk tip bundle; first individual transaction in a bundle, besides trunk tip, also directly approves branch tip – the last individual transaction in another (previous) bundle called branch tip bundle.
Lazy Tip	A tip, i.e., an older transaction in the Tangle selected for approval (by the newest transaction), which had already been approved by other old transactions that came after.
LIDAR	A method for measuring distances (ranging) by illuminating the target with laser light and measuring the reflection with a sensor.
Litecoin	A blockchain-based cryptocurrency created and launched by Charlie Lee in 2011; it differs from Bitcoins in aspects like faster block generation rate and use of script algorithm as PoW, which requires much more memory than Bitcoin's hash-hash PoW algorithm; Litecoin is often mentioned as the silver to Bitcoin's gold.
Machine to Machine Communication	Direct communication between devices using any communications channel, including wired and wireless.

Man-in-the-Middle Attack	An attack where the attacker secretly relays and possibly alters the communications between two parties who believe that they are directly communicating with each other.
Master Shard	Entity (of the Hedera platform) that controls the allocation of nodes to different shards.
Merkle Tree	A hash-based data structure with tree topology, i.e., a generalization of the hash list in which each leaf node is a hash of a block of data, and each non-leaf node is a hash of its children; Merkle trees typically have a branching factor of 2, meaning that each node has up to 2 children.
Meta Transaction (in a bundle)	An individual transaction (in a bundle) with the neutral (zero) value written in the field Value; meta transactions are used as extensions of input transactions, usually having the tail parts of the input transactions' signatures.
Milestone (in the context of Tangle)	A transaction in the Tangle issued by the IOTA Foundation as a guarantee that all transactions approved directly or indirectly by this transaction are immediately considered as part of the consensus.
Miner	A participant/node in the blockchain's P2P network involved in the blockchain mining process, in which miners try to solve a computationally intensive task (typically a mathematical problem or puzzle) in order to gain the opportunity to add a new block of transactions to the blockchain, and as a reward, to earn a certain amount of cryptocurrency (defined by the applied blockchain algorithm), as well as to get the transactions' fees.
Mining Pool	A joint group of cryptocurrency miners, who combine their computational resources over a network in order to solve a PoW task and add a block of transactions to the blockchain; if the pool does the PoW successfully, it is rewarded with cryptocurrency tokens; the reward is divided to the miners who contributed according to the proportion of each miner's processing power or work relative to the whole group.
Multi-homing	The practice of connecting a host or a computer network to more than one network. Most commonly, it is done to increase reliability or performance.
Node	A participant in the P2P network of a particular blockchain on which is run the blockchain's native coin/cryptocurrency or decentralized application.
Nonce	Abbreviation for the number only used once that blockchain miners are solving, i.e., searching for, before adding a new block to the blockchain; it is a 32-bit value put in the header of a transaction block (of the Bitcoin blockchain) which meets the difficulty level restrictions in the sense that the 256-bit hash value of the block header (with the nonce included) is small enough, i.e., that has a required number of leading binary zeros; for each block, the hash value of the block header (containing

Other-parent Event	The last event created earlier by the hashgraph node, which sent a new gossip/sync message (to the node, which then creates a new event).
Output Transaction (in a bundle)	An individual transaction (in a bundle) with the Value field that contains a positive value, which represents the amount of IOTAs that is to be added to the account specified by the field Address.
Partition Attack	A type of attack on the Bitcoin's P2P network in which an adversary (e.g., a malicious transit autonomous system on the Internet) exploits vulnerabilities of Border Gateway Protocol and performs prefix hijacking of a part of the P2P network, i.e., isolates a group of victim nodes (of the Bitcoin's P2P network) in a certain point of the Internet; the consequence is that all blocks (and transactions contained within) solved during isolation period by the victim nodes will be discarded after the end of isolation because, after that, the blockchain version maintained on the victim nodes cannot survive in the whole network (due to smaller hash power of victim nodes compared to the rest of the network).
Peer-to-Peer network	A network of equally privileged nodes (peers) connected by means of direct links, all of them participating in a decentralized application.
Permissioned DL	A distributed ledger in which each network participant (node) needs permission from a central entity (e.g., owner or administrator of the ledger) to access the network and make changes, i.e., to add transactions to the ledger.
Permissionless DL	A distributed ledger without a central owner that controls network access, so any participant may join the network and add transactions to the ledger if the participant (computer node) runs the relevant software that complies with the rules of the applied consensus mechanism.
Proof of Capacity	See Proof of Space
Proof of Space	Also called Proof of Storage or Proof of Capacity; the concept originally introduced for showing that one has a legitimate interest in service by allocating a sufficient amount of memory or disk space to solve a challenge presented by the service provider; it can be used as consensus mechanism as well, for achieving distributed consensus among the members/nodes of a cryptocurrency blockchain P2P network.
Proof of Stake	A type of consensus mechanism, i.e., an algorithm for achieving distributed consensus (among the members/nodes of a cryptocurrency blockchain P2P network) where the winner, i.e., the creator of the next transaction block (that is to be added to the blockchain), is chosen among the blockchain community members in dependence of the members' stakes (the amounts of cryptocurrency members posses).

Proof of Work	A type of consensus mechanism, i.e., an algorithm for achieving distributed consensus (among the members/nodes of a cryptocurrency blockchain P2P network) that requires some work from the service requester, usually meaning processing time by a computer while solving a given mathematical problem, a computationally intensive puzzle, etc.
Random Walk Monte Carlo Algorithm	Algorithm for selection of a tip that will be approved by a new transaction that should be added to the Tangle.
Round (in the context of hashgraph)	A part (a portion of events) that the hashgraph diagram is divided into as it grows in time.
Round Created (of an event)	A serial number of the round an event belongs to in the hashgraph diagram; round created of an event is calculated as follows: if the event strongly sees a supermajority of witnesses of round r, where r is the max of the round created of the event's parents, then the round created of the event is r+1 (otherwise, round created of the event is r).
Round Received (of an event)	A serial number of the first round after an event (in the hashgraph diagram) which fulfills the condition that all the famous witnesses of that round see this event (not necessarily strongly); in other words, if an event is seen by all round n famous witnesses, this event is said to be received (by the community of nodes) in round n, i.e., that it has round received of n.
Seeing (in the context of hashgraph)	A situation (in the hashgraph diagram) when an event Y is linked with some previous event X via at least one path no matter through how many nodes the path passes.
Segregated Witness Protocol	A protocol upgrade of the Bitcoin blockchain that enables protection from transaction malleability and increases the block size limit (from 1MB to a little under 4MB) on the blockchain by removing signature data from Bitcoin transactions.
Self-parent Event	The previous event created by the hashgraph node, which receives a new gossip/sync message (and creates a new event).
Shards/Sharding Architecture	The architecture (i.e., the arrangement) of the Hedera platform nodes that should enable scalability and continuous decentralization of the platform in the future; the architecture assumes the existence of shards (partitions, groups) of nodes, where each shard contains a relatively small number of nodes.
Site (in the context of Tangle)	Graph representation of a transaction in Tangle (issued by a node of IOTA network).
Smart Car	In the past, this term denoted a car with advanced electronics; now (and in a stricter sense), a smart car is the car that, besides numerous enhancements, also possesses a property to be highly interconnected (e.g., via WiFi, Bluetooth, 4G/5G) and with a certain level of self-driving automation capabilities (from assisted driving to the fully autonomous driving).

Smart Contract	Computer code running on a DLT platform; it executes automatically when specific conditions are met; due to the execution on a DLT platform, a smart contract runs exactly as programmed (according to the agreed contract terms), i.e., there is no chance of being changed, interrupted, censored or interfered by any third party; smart contract execution enables the exchange of value.
Smart Factory	A highly digitalized and connected environment where machinery and equipment are able to improve processes through automation and self-optimization.
Smart Manufacturing	This term is practically synonymous with Industry 4.0, which gives solutions involving one or more technologies such are: Internet of Things, Artificial Intelligence, Augmented Reality, Automation/Robotics, or Additive manufacturing/3D printing.
Solidified Block	A block in a blockchain, after which were added a few (i.e., less than 6) new blocks.
Solidity (programming language)	Programming language for smart contracts; initially developed for the execution of smart contracts on the Ethereum platform.
Strongly Seeing (in the context of hashgraph)	A situation (in the hashgraph diagram) when an event Y is linked with some previous event X in a way that all paths that connect X and Y contain (in whole) a supermajority of nodes (including the nodes that created events X and Y).
Supermajority (in the context of hashgraph)	Any group of hashgraph nodes that gathers more than 2/3 of the total number of nodes.
Sybil Attack	Type of attack where attacker subverts the reputation system of network service by creating a large number of pseudonymous identities and uses them to gain a disproportionately large influence; named after the subject of the book Sybil, a case study of a woman diagnosed with a dissociative identity disorder.
Tangle/IOTA	A distributed ledger project that logically relies on a new DAG structure (called Tangle), designed to record and execute transactions between machines and devices in the IoT ecosystem, realizing its native token (cryptocurrency) called IOTA.
Target_value	A parameter that represents the upper limit under which the 256-bit hash value should be found for successful verification of a new block.
Tip	A (relatively new) transaction previously added to the Tangle, which is selected to be directly approved by a new transaction.
TLS Encryption	Abbreviation from Transport Layer Security – a cryptographic protocol designed to provide communications security (primarily privacy and data integrity) between two or more communicating computer applications over a network; TLS operates on top of Transmission Control Protocol.
Transaction	A sequence of information exchange between communication partners.

Transaction block	A block (i.e., set) of transactions – the basic data structure/unit which is linked with other blocks in a series by means of cryptography, creating that way a blockchain.
Transaction Fee (or Miner Fee)	The fee paid (in cryptocurrency) by the purchaser within a transaction to a miner who verified this transaction (i.e., who added the transaction onto blockchain); with Bitcoin blockchain, a miner who successfully adds a block of transactions to the blockchain gets the fees for all transactions in the block.
Tritt	A digit in balanced ternary logic; can take values from set {+1, 0, −1}.
Trunk Tip	A tip that represents the last individual transaction in a trunk tip bundle (see IOTA bundle).
Trustless Truth	A term that denotes the state of a community in which exists a general consensus about something (e.g., about the trust in Bitcoin), where no one trusts anyone and where (just because of overall distrust) a set of rules (or a mechanism like PoW) is imposed to all participants, achieving in that way that eventually, everyone is confident about some common thing of interest.
Tryte	A word of 3 Tritts (in balanced ternary logic); for designation of Trytes in IOTA (27 different values) are used 26 uppercase letters "A", "B", "C", . . ., "X", "Y", "Z" and symbol "9" (which in balanced ternary logic represents the value +1).
Vehicle-to-Environment (or Vehicle-to-Everything) Communication	Passing of information from a vehicle to any entity that may affect the vehicle, and vice versa; it is a vehicular communication system that incorporates other more specific types of communication as Vehicle-to-Infrastructure, Vehicle-to-Network, Vehicle-to-Vehicle, Vehicle-to-Pedestrian, Vehicle-to-Device and Vehicle-to-Grid.
Virtual Voting (in the context of hashgraph)	A voting process in which the community (i.e., the nodes of hashgraph P2P network) collectively and democratically establishes the consensus on the transactions' order in time; it is called virtual because nodes do not really send their votes over the Internet (i.e., the Yes/No decisions regarding the so-called famous witnesses), but each node calculates what votes other nodes would have sent, based on its knowledge of what other nodes know.
Vote Weighting	An adjustment of virtual voting algorithm realized with the aim to enable usage of the algorithm in the community (of members/ hashgraph nodes) whose members are not equal and where the significance of a member depends on the stake (the amount of Hedera's native tokens) the member possesses; the adjustment is made through simple redefinitions of notions of majority, supermajority, and median value, whereby the members' stakes are taken into account.
Witness of a Round (in the context of hashgraph)	An event (at the beginning of a round) that strongly sees a supermajority of witnesses from the previous round; witnesses of round 1 are the first events ever created by the corresponding nodes.

1 Distributed ledger technologies

Distributed Ledger Technologies (DLTs) enable an innovative special form of electronic data processing and its memorizing. As the main part, a distributed ledger is a decentralized database that allows all the members of a concerned network to read and write data in it. Unlike centralized databases, no central instance allowing data writing and reading is needed here. Instead of having a centralized control, any network member can add data anytime, after which a process of data actualization follows. Each network member is provided with the newest up-to-date state of a database.

As DLTs reduce the cost of trust and revolutionize transactions between individuals, companies, and governments and minimize successful frauds, error possibility, and paper-intensive processes, they are considered a progressive technology of the future. They can have a crucial impact on society in every respect, especially in machine-to-machine (M2M) communications, one of the basic technologies for the Internet of Things (IoT). Besides providing security, privacy, and decentralized operation, DLTs stand for reliable, autonomous, and trusted IoT platforms now and in the future.

DLT follows a new data recording, sharing, and synchronizing method across multiple ledgers (data stores). A distributed ledger (DL) is a database that is independently created, maintained, and updated by each node (or participant) in a large network. All the records of a distributed ledger are shared and synchronized by consensus between nodes across the network. This happens without the help of any central authority. Consequently, each network node has its ledger copy, identical to others. Every time the ledger has to be updated with the new record(s), reaching a consensus results in getting identical copies on all nodes. This synchronization process is very fast, so that changes in a node's ledger are copied into the ledgers on other nodes in just a few seconds (or perhaps minutes).

Cryptographic signatures are used to secure access to the ledger's content, so that all DL data is accurate and safe. In many cases, to succeed in a cyberattack, an attacker has to target most DL copies simultaneously. Besides, if one or few copies are corrupted, the system as a whole will not be compromised.

Any node may create a data block with which the actual will be updated. Then, the information (created block) is broadcast across the network, after which other nodes check its validity through a consensus mechanism, that is, pre-defined validation method. After the community (i.e., a valid majority of network nodes) has validated a new block, each node, that is, participant, adds it to its copy of the ledger.

As for consensus mechanisms, there are several of them, such as a Proof of Work (PoW), Proof of Stake (PoS), Proof of Space (PoSpace), and so on. PoW can be the solution to a mathematical problem or puzzle or a suitable hash value found through the iterative execution of the appropriate hash function.

https://doi.org/10.1515/9783110681130-001

A consensus accomplished by PoS is a process in which a new block is validated only by the participants having enough high stakes, that is, by the rich members. They have many native tokens (cryptocurrency) of a concrete DL on their accounts. The PoS concept is based on the idea that the trustworthiness in the network (and in the value of token) decreases if everyone could perform block validations, which consequently increases the possibility of validation of illegitimate blocks. Hence, the only way of keeping the system's trust is by leaving the block validation to in the members who might lose much money if acting in irresponsible ways. Regarding energy consumption, PoS is faster and more efficient than PoW (but less proven).

In the PoSpace concept, the available space (memory) on hard discs of the miners' computers is the resource used for mining (instead of computational power used with PoW). It is also called Proof of Capacity (PoC). Compared to PoW, this concept also saves time and energy. PoSpace is a good solution for anti-spam measures and the prevention of DoS attacks. It could also be useful in preventing the centralization of mining power in mining pools.

There are two types of DLs: public and private, depending on the peer-to-peer (P2P) network they rely on. Based on control by certain entities, there are also two types of DLs: permissionless and permissioned. In a permissionless DL, each node of the network hosts the full and freshest copy of the complete ledger. Every ledger update (addition of a new block) is communicated to all nodes in the network, which then collectively validate the new block by obeying a consensus mechanism. Having accepted the validation, a new block is added to each node's copy of the ledger. Data consistency across the network is assured in that way. This means that a permissionless DL is fully democratic and with no central control, provided each participant follows the predefined rules. In a permissioned DL, however, a central entity grants the permissions to nodes for accessing the network and making changes to the ledger. At the same time, the central entity can also verify the identity of the participants who try to access the network.

As there are a number of DLT applications that boost autonomous driving, this chapter will consider basic DLT architectures and their properties and several use cases of these technologies in the concept of autonomous vehicles.

Three basic DLT architectures will be considered for comparing DLT characteristics in the remaining part of the paper: chain or list, Directed Acyclic Graph (DAG) as a tangle, and DAG as a tree. A typical representative of the chain or list is a blockchain, which is the basis for the oldest and most widely used cryptocurrency – the Bitcoin (BTC), invented in 2008 by Satoshi Nakamoto [1]. DAG is a finite directed graph with no directed cycles and consists of many finite vertices and edges. Each edge is directed from one vertex to another but with no back loops. Tangle is a basis for IOTA, a cryptocurrency that is one of the main concurrences of the BTC, especially in the field of M2M communications. IOTA was founded in 2015 by David Sonstebo, Sergey Ivancheglo, Dominik Schiener, and Serguei Popov [2] and has worked formally as IOTA Foundation since 2017. DAG as a tree is the newest DLT architecture, which is the basis for the so-called hashgraph. Hashgraph is a data structure that records the data about who gossiped with whom and in which order. US professor Leemon Baird invented hashgraph in 2016 [3].

1.1 Digital money – cryptocurrencies

DLTs are widely used in the financial sector as cryptocurrencies or crypto money. These days, the world is witnessing the true gold rush for cryptocurrencies. Many of those involved in the so-called easy money business related to DLTs understand how cryptocurrencies work. Still, others ask a simple question: "How is it possible to make real money from nothing?" Jokes are made comparing cryptocurrencies with some modern physicists' hypothesis that the whole universe came from nothing. So, if this applies to the universe, why could it not be applied to cryptocurrencies, too?

These are other most often asked questions: "How come the whole system is still functioning?," "Is it a kind of fraud?," "How long will it last?," "Why do people believe in digital money when there is no supreme authority to guarantee it?," "Is the whole thing and the euphoria related to this only one of the numerous economic bubbles with the growing mechanism based on human greed, with the inevitable final collapse?," and so on.

And yet, many financial experts foresee a bright future of cryptocurrencies and a further evolution of DLTs. They say that they will enable numerous services such as absolute trust, security, and transparency, showing the way to the societies that have a high level of justice, without criminal and corruption, that is, to the societies that many utopists had only been dreaming of.

Let us remember some of the facts about money: the first forms of human transactions were in pieces of a material (e.g., copper, silver, or gold) which had a value by itself. For example, gold was (and still is) a precious metal due to its characteristics that make it suitable for various applications. For this reason, people believed (and they still do) that the value of gold can be exchanged for other goods, that is, used for trading, while being aware that it could be turned into a useful or a beautiful and valuable object. The keyword here is trust, that is, the faith in the value of the objects named coins or money.

This faith in coins can be (and many times in history was) jeopardized by making coins with a certain (often unknown) percentage of other materials of lesser worth, making unfair trade and fraudulent behavior quite possible in that manner. The natural evolutionary step was to ensure a community where each used coin is worth the labeled value. Only a few powerful central authorities could have obtained such an assurance (e.g., emperors, kings, governments, and other community rulers). The guarantee mechanism was based on the monopoly of money production, the power and reputation of the authority, and the insurance measures (using advanced technology of the time) taken to make money difficult to forge by common people. Suppose the aforementioned conditions are fulfilled to some extent, it can be said that there is an informal agreement in the community that a given currency can be used for trading. The key terms related to real money that should be remembered, here, are central authority and its reputation.

Money is a dynamic category whose value can vary very much, depending on many factors (e.g., inflation). All conditions are not always needed for general consent on the money value. There were some specific circumstances (in history) in some places where central authority had not guaranteed the value of money. Still, the trust in the means of payment had been achieved due to the peculiarities or rareness of the things and objects found in nature, which had been used then for trading, for example, bear claws or shells.

An interesting example is the use of huge and immovable sacred stones as money in a few isolated Pacific islands. The stones had been changing hands after each transaction between tribe members. The ownership of each stone was carved on it as in a ledger (wordings show similarity with today's ledgers).

It is useful to draw a parallel and note a distinction between cryptocurrency and paper money. Taken by itself, a piece of paper almost has no value. Yet, banknotes, pieces of paper have definite values as the central bank of a country, the authority which issued them, guarantees (by its assets or by the reserves in gold, or even by the reputation of their country), that each banknote can be changed for a piece of gold or another thing of a certain value. Each banknote should represent a certain amount of gold that the bank has saved in its vaults, and it was the case from the very beginning. But it is known that for a long time, many currencies (including the US Dollar, the British Pound, and the Euro) have no gold coverage – they are called fiat currencies. Despite this fact, these currencies are (more or less) concurrent and worthy at their markets. The trust in a currency generally depends on the strength of the country's economy, reputation, and many other factors. The similarity between a cryptocurrency and a fiat currency is that their value is based on the trust in the system, while the mechanisms which keep that trust differ.

Another new phenomenon has emerged in recent years: paper money and coins are not being used in many countries. Plastic or virtual money (through debit/credit cards and gadgets) is broadly adopted instead, now, and real money has its material representative, no more. Still, it is stored as information in the computer systems of banks holding the customers' accounts. From their side, banks guarantee (with their reputation, as the recognized authorities) that the stored information on the account states of their customers are true.

Taking into consideration all the above-exposed facts, we could think of cryptocurrencies as not so strange. Even more – they may look like the next natural evolutionary step in the story of money.

1.2 Blockchain

Blockchain is a reliable transaction register (or ledger) containing all transactions up to this very moment. It is a big and continuously growing file comprising a list of records called blocks (or blocks of transactions) where each block in the list is linked (i.e., chained) with the previous and the next block, using cryptography (see Fig. 1.1). The key conditions are that besides transaction data, each block has a header that contains a cryptographic hash of the previous block's header, a timestamp that transactions relate to, and six other fields (if the Bitcoin blockchain [1] is concerned; see Fig. 1.2).

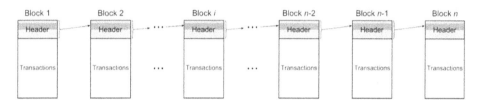

Fig. 1.1: BTC blockchain – line topology.

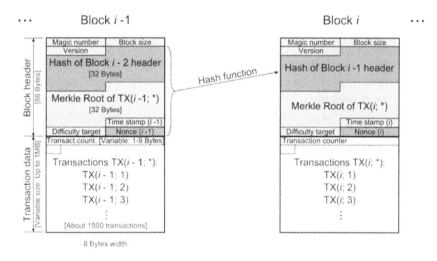

Fig. 1.2: Structure of a block and connection with the next block in the BTC blockchain.

Let us suppose that a BTC blockchain (just one of the cryptocurrencies using blockchain technology) records all BTC transactions that people have ever made. In other words, blockchain is a financial book with precise and reliable data on all past transactions of money (between community members) from the very beginning. Or even simpler said – blockchain is a reliable transaction register (or ledger) that contains all transactions up to this very moment. It is a big and continuously growing file. For example, a BTC blockchain (each cryptocurrency has its blockchain, just like Bitcoin), now, has a few hundreds of GB and records all BTC transactions between people.

The key point of the whole system is that no one can ever delete or modify any of these transactions, and this is the main reason why blockchain has become a hot topic. It offers absolute permanency and reliability of the recorded data, so that no hacker can get into this blockchain database and change the fact that, for instance, John Smith possesses 20 BTCs. Such properties of BTC are accomplished by two most significant factors:

1. Decentralization
2. The algorithm for the verification of transactions, which is closely related to the blockchain structure

The concept of decentralization is achieved when the list of all transactions (blockchain) is stored in many computers worldwide, where each of these computers (called nodes) contains a file of the complete blockchain (which should be identical to the blockchain file of any other node). Unlike centralized banking systems where each bank keeps customers' transaction data on its servers (well protected and backed up), the nodes keeping a blockchain belong to ordinary people all over the world, who have accepted to take part in this DL voluntarily. There is neither a central authority nor a central register to keep data. People with node computers are mutually independent, except that their computers host the nodes that maintain a blockchain. Nodes are always connected using a protocol for inter-node communication, thus creating a global peer-to-peer (P2P) network. However, this network is like any other P2P network running over the Internet.

A fresh copy of the file of blockchain is kept on the disk of each node. Besides, some nodes (miners) can also verify the newest transactions (e.g., in BTCs) between any two people in the world. Furthermore, there are many other computers with only a transaction verification function. They are also called miners, although they are not nodes.

Let us take the following example: A wants to send 100 EUR (in BTCs) to B: in the beginning, a computer (or a smartphone) of A announces to all miners in the network that A wants to transfer 100 EUR to B. At that moment, this is called an invalidated transaction, and it is not written into the register yet.

The first thing for a miner to do next is check if A has enough money (at least 100 EUR and something more for the provision). Now, the miner checks this by passing through the complete blockchain, seeing all transactions that person A has ever had, and calculating if there is enough money available. As there is no such category as the account state, the amount of money A possesses is always counted again, based on all the transactions A has ever had up to that moment. That is a very favorable trait, making the blockchain additionally safe. If one wanted to manipulate another person's account, one would have to change the transactions from the past, which is impossible.

Having finished this (easier) first step, that is, the confirmation of A's solvency, the second and more difficult step follows. There, miners compete with each other: the winner is the first one managing to embed the new transaction; that is, to append it to the end of the blockchain.

Only one particular transaction has been mentioned so far (between person A and person B) as the single one, which should be validated and added to the blockchain. In reality, a block that is to be appended to the end of the BTC blockchain contains, on average, 1,500 transactions accumulated from around the world in ten minutes. In general, for different types of the blockchain (other than BTC blockchain), the frequency of appearance of new blocks is different, so there are blockchains where one block of transactions appears even every five seconds.

The transaction data of each block (of the BTC blockchain) consists of the latest valid transactions, whereby the size of the block is limited to 1 MB (although with the use of Segregated Witness protocol upgrade [4] from August 2017, block limit has been extended to 4 MB, for practical purposes). The participants' identities in a transaction are encrypted prior, using their private keys. All transactions in a block are hashed through a cryptographic scheme known as a hash tree or Merkle tree [5]. The 256-bit long result of hashing, that is, the root of the Merkle tree, is put into the block header as well.

The links between blocks make a blockchain practically unbreakable, as each block contains the hash value of the previous block's header. The catch is in the 32-bit block header field named nonce (from number-used-once), the value of which all the miners in the world are trying to guess every ten minutes, to append a new block to the blockchain (and, consequently, to get a reward for the invested work, if successful). Once a new block is put to the blockchain, all the transactions from that block are considered verified, and miners immediately go on finding new nonce for the next block of transactions. The first miner who verifies these transactions by guessing the right value of nonce (in the previous block) gets a reward. With a BTC blockchain, the reward consists of two parts – the first is a transaction fee, paid in BTCs by money-transaction senders from the just verified block, and the second part is a certain amount of new BTCs generated from nothing.

What is the right value of nonce? There is no such value, that is, no tangible value has been set in advance. More specifically, the algorithm is designed, so that the goal to be achieved is to adjust the hash value of the last verified block header in blockchain to be small enough, that is, to be less than or equal to a given number (target). This practically means that this hash value, which is to be put in the header of the next (i.e., of the newest) block, begins with several zeros. The adjustment of the hash value is performed through an iterative process of incrementing the value of nonce and computing a new hash (of the complete block header) for each new nonce. The process stops when the currently computed hash satisfies the given condition.

Knowing the properties of the cryptographic hash functions (in the case of BTC, SHA-256 algorithm is used, i.e., the hash is 256 bits long), it is obvious that the probability of guessing a hash with a given number of leading zeros is extremely small (in one attempt). If the goal (for a given level of difficulty) is to compute a hash where, for example, the first 72 bits are zeros (or in hexadecimal notation: hash = 00000000 00000000 00xxxxxx xxxxxxxx xxxxxxxx xxxxxxxx xxxxxxxx xxxxxxxx), and assuming a uniform distribution of hash values, the probability of success in one attempt would be $2^{-72} = 1/4,722,000,000,000,000,000,000$. With such a small probability, the time needed for a specialized mining computer (e.g., with the processing power of 16 Thash/s) to solely find the winning combination of nonce and hash would be more than nine years, by a rough estimate! Still, on average, a new block is being added to the blockchain every ten minutes. How is it achieved?

The answer is in the enormous processing power obtained by the combined effort of the computers of all miners in the world. The precise number of BTC miners is difficult to be determined, as it is always changing, with a growing trend. When they are not mining BTCs, many of them use their computers for mining other cryptocurrencies as well, and a few are mining from time to time, for example, during the time intervals when a miner's computer is not used for playing games. Eventually, the exact number of miners is not very important, as the processing powers of their computers are different. On the other hand, however, it all depends on the miners' readiness to invest in hardware, together with all expenses for electric power, among others.

These days, a great number of miners are gathered in mining pools, as they are aware that mining solely is not profitable, because a block's verification process would take an unacceptably long time. Mining pools are joint groups of miners that acquire advantages such as much more frequent verifications of transaction blocks. Miners from a pool share the rewards for successful verifications, proportional to the miners' mining powers contributed to the pool. Apart from that, most BTC mining is done on the Application Specific Integrated Circuits (ASICs) in large, thermally-regulated data centers and warehouses with low-cost electricity. The owners of such warehouses rent the processing resources to miners.

As the world's mining power is increasingly growing, the same is expected from the frequency of block verifications and the acceleration of BTCs' issuance. But these have not happened yet, due to the applied algorithm known as Difficulty, which adjusts the difficulty level for solving the verification problem. The algorithm keeps the average block verification frequency almost constant. A new block is added to the blockchain every 10 min approximately, or more precisely – within two weeks, 2016 blocks should be added to the blockchain. Every two weeks, the algorithm changes the value of the block header field named Difficulty target (Fig. 1.2), according to the statistics of the total mining power and the number of transactions.

The value of the 32-bit Difficulty target field corresponds (in a bit more complex way) to the difficulty of finding the hash, which is small enough to satisfy the condition for block verification. It has been mentioned earlier that the hash value written in the verified block must be less than or equal to a given value, called target_value (in Fig. 1.3 named X). A reference value called difficulty_1_target is also defined to

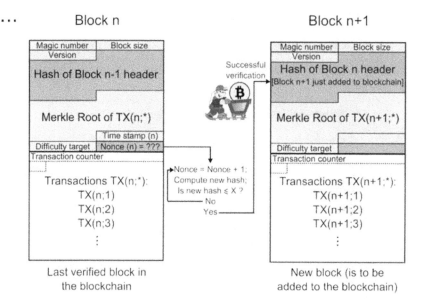

Fig. 1.3: Adding of a new block at the end of the BTC blockchain.

represent the 256-bit number, where the leading 32 bits are zero, the next 16 bits are one, and the rest are zero, or in hexadecimal notation:

$$difficulty\_1\_target = 00000000ffff0000\ 00000000\ 00000000\ 00000000$$
$$00000000\ 00000000\ 00000000$$
$$= ffff_{(hex)} \times 2^{208}{}_{(dec)} = 2^{16} \times 2^{208} = 2^{224} \qquad (1.1)$$

A parameter known as Difficulty is defined as:

$$Difficulty = difficulty\_1\_target / target\_value \qquad (1.2)$$

Thus, it shows how many times it is more difficult to find a hash below the current target value than to find a hash below difficulty_1_target. The Difficulty is a floating-point value, and in the Difficulty target field of the block header, it is represented by exponent and mantissa of the target_value, where the first 8 bits are exponent. The rest of the 24 bits are mantissa. If, for example, target_value (in hexadecimal notation) is "172*f4f7b*", the following predefined formula should be used to calculate the target_value of hash:

$$target\_value = \mathbf{2f4f7b} \cdot 2^{8 \cdot (17-3)}{}_{(hex)} =$$

$$00000000\ 00000000\ 00\mathbf{2f4f7b}00000000\ 00000000$$
$$00000000\ 00000000\ 00000000 \qquad (1.3)$$

and using (1) and (2) we have the result for Difficulty (in decimals):

$$\text{Difficulty} = 5,949,437,371,609.53 \approx 5.95 \times 10^{12} \text{(or 5.95 T)} \tag{1.4}$$

The number of leading binary zeros in the target_value of hash can be calculated from Difficulty as:

$$\text{Number of leading zeros} = \log_2(\text{Difficulty}) + 32 \tag{1.5}$$

In this example, the result is 74.44. This can also be seen from the hexadecimal representation of target_value in (3), where the first 18 nibbles (4-bit blocks) represent 72 binary zeros, and the next nibble $2_{(hex)} = 0010_{(bin)}$ adds two more zeros, which, on the whole, gives 74 leading zeros.

Suppose we want to assure that a block is verified every 10 min. In that case, Difficulty should be tuned relative to the computational power of the entire Bitcoin network, so that it can make a targeted number of calculations per second needed for achieving of the goal that average time for finding a hash below or equal to target_value is ten minutes. This number of hash operations per second (known as hash power or hash rate) can be derived and calculated from Difficulty as follows:

$$\text{Hash rate} = \frac{\{N(\text{Difficulty})\}}{10min} \tag{1.6}$$

where $\{N(\text{Difficulty})\}$ is the expected number of hash attempts (for a given Difficulty) before finding a valid hash:

$$\{N(\text{Difficulty})\} = \frac{2^{256}}{\text{target\_value}} \tag{1.7}$$

By combining (2), (6), and (7), we have:

$$\text{Hash rate} = \frac{1}{10min} \cdot \frac{2^{256}}{\dfrac{\text{difficulty\_1\_target}}{\text{Difficulty}}} = \frac{1}{600s} \cdot \frac{2^{256}}{2^{224}} \cdot \text{Difficulty} = \text{Difficulty} \cdot 2^{32}/600s$$

$$\tag{1.8}$$

For example, if Difficulty = 5.95 T, using (1.8), the hash rate is 42,587,731,567,771, 900,000 hashes/s, that is, 42.6 Exahash per second (42.6 EH/s). With the same Difficulty, a computer with 16 TH/s processing power should be mining for around 50 years to find a solution (time = 600s × 42.6EH/s / 16TH/s).

This huge Difficulty makes it easier to find a particular sand grain among all of Earth's sand grains than to find a successful hash. Mining pools can find a solution in about ten minutes due to their appropriate hash power. However, the disadvantage is the enormous consumption of (electric) energy. Currently, the total power spent by all Bitcoin miners in the world equals the energy consumption of a developed country. So, a logical question comes up: Why is it all necessary? Why the mining algorithm is designed that way, that is, with the artificially added computational difficulty?

1.2.1 Concept of proof of work

The answer to the previous questions and to how new BTCs are issued can be found in the applied concept, PoW. The PoW concept is used for maintaining blockchain (DL) consistent, strong and unbreakable, which are key factors that create trustworthiness of the whole system and consensus in the community about the real value of cryptocurrency.

The concept of PoW is not new. It has been used in computer networks with client–server mechanisms as a measure to discourage Denial of Service (DoS) attacks and other abuses such as spam. The main property of PoW is its asymmetry – a client's relatively hard work when compared to the ease with which the result can be checked by a server. In the case of a BTC blockchain, the result of the very difficult job of finding a valid nonce-hash pair by a successful miner (i.e., mining pool) is very easily confirmed by other miners.

It has already been mentioned that the trustworthiness of the BTC also contributed to the decentralization of the blockchain. Let us remember that the BTC blockchain, as a DL of transaction blocks is realized using nodes, that is the computers connected to the BTC P2P network. BTC full nodes are the computers running the BTC Core client with the complete blockchain. A transaction is a process of sending BTCs from the BTC wallet (i.e., address) of a sender to the BTC wallet of a person who receives money. Money senders broadcast transactions to the network. Full nodes validate transactions and relay them to other nodes by broadcasting messages across the network. Within this decentralized infrastructure (P2P network), a set of miners collect transaction records, verify that each transaction is signed correctly and is not in conflict with previous transactions. They also check that the sender (whose identity is hidden behind an address) does not move more BTCs than is contained in the address (passing through the entire blockchain) and perform other functions.

Each miner independently collects valid transactions and aggregates them into a candidate block. Then, a miner attempts to solve his candidate block through the PoW, that is, through the process of finding a valid hash (as described in Section 1.2). The first miner who successfully solves a candidate block broadcasts his solution to the network (including other miners) to be added to the blockchain. The key thing here is that the new block will be added to the blockchain only if more than 50% of miners say it has been solved correctly. And before saying that, miners have to make their calculations on the solved block, comparing their results to the solution that was broadcast. Two different candidate blocks may be solved at about the same time. In that situation, two solutions will propagate through the network (this situation is known as a blockchain fork). Still, eventually, only one will win, that is, it will be added to the blockchain (the first accepted by most miners). At the same time, the other solved block (the orphan) will stale, and the transactions from this block (the ones which are not included in the winning block) will wait for the next round, to be collected and verified within some of the forthcoming candidate blocks. The triggering moment for the decision of which of two solutions will win is after about 10 min, when the next block is added the first time (somewhere in the network) on top of the winning block. Then, the newly added block will be broadcast as the solution (where the previous winning block is included in the blockchain). The community will quickly accept it, assuming that the last added block was the only offered solution at the moment, which is the most common case.

Having received the news that the candidate block has been solved, a miner should only verify that the solution is correct, as the solution is already known. However, although a solved block can be added to the blockchain only if it is verified by at least 50% of miners, they do not have to verify it. A miner first decides whether it should wait to verify the block before starting on the next block or start immediately with solving the next block, assuming the previous block was correct. The benefit of making the assumption is that there will not be any wasted time spent on verification, which increases the profit by about 10%. As a result, many large mining pools skip this verification process and, just using the newly appended blockchain, immediately start working on the next block.

Using a procedure involving PoW and the consensus of more than half of the participants, the so-called trustless truth is accomplished. Trustless truth is a term that denotes the state of a community where there is a consensus about something (here, about the trust in the BTC), whereby no one trusts anyone. Nevertheless, just because of this overall distrust, a set of rules (or a mechanism like PoW) is imposed on all participants. Eventually, everyone is confident about some common thing of interest.

In this case, the BTC blockchain is such a giant and reliable data structure, just because of the huge amount of computational work needed for its growth. This work (due to general distrust) must be proven through PoW and verified by the majority of miners. If someone tried to change (i.e., forge) some of the previous transactions, just to change the state of someone's digital wallet, he would have to create a new consistent version of the blockchain (with one changed block). It would have to pass the verification process by the miners' community. Changing a block inside the blockchain (which can only be done by making a new block containing the same predecessor) requires regenerating all successor blocks and redoing all the work they contain. This is practically impossible due to the tremendous work the forger would have to do, on its own. The more blocks in the blockchain after the targeted block there are, the more difficult it is to create some other version of the blockchain, which the targeted block tampers with. In this way, a decentralized system with incorporated trustless truth mechanisms gains the reputation of the monetary authority that only some centralized monetary institutions, for example, central banks in various countries enjoy,. Furthermore, the BTC has become a global monetary system that is not under the control of any government or any central authority.

Apart from decentralization and PoW mechanism, the reason for such a sustainable development and value for the BTC also lies in the monetary policy, that is, in the policy of BTC issuance. It is the main motivating factor (the incentive) for the army of miners worldwide to do the transaction verification job. Although it seems now that every 10 min, a new number of BTCs appears out of thin air in the ever continuing process of block solving, the BTC, still, has no inflationary character – that is, the total amount of BTCs is limited by its design, which is why it is often called digital gold.

BTC is the oldest and most known digital currency launched on the Internet in 2009. Now, it cannot exceed a total amount of 21 million (precisely: 20,999,999.9769 BTC). In the beginning, the reward for solving the block was 50 BTC, and the Difficulty of the opening blocks in the blockchain was 1, that is, the hashes were with only 8 leading binary zeros. As said before, the Difficulty of block solving adjusts every 2016 blocks, that is, about every 14 days, depending on the miners' total computation power. The BTC block reward halves every 210,000 blocks. Currently, the reward is 6.25 BTC and was last halved from 12.5 BTC with block 630,000 on May 27, 2020. Many miners may leave the job after that because of their reduced profit, but on the other hand, with miners' reduced power, the Difficulty will be reduced accordingly. Consequently, less electricity will be required to mine each new BTC.

Lastly, let us point out that by the year 2032, almost all BTCs will have been mined when the reward would drop below 1 BTC, and the only incentive of the miners (if anyone remains) will be the transaction fees. But it is not possible to have precise predictions about the BTC's future and survival by that time, after all.

1.2.2 Vulnerabilities of the BTC and issues handling

Even before the BTC, there had been attempts to create sustainable digital money. All the attempts had failed because there were no reliable mechanisms to successfully prevent scenarios in which transactions are copied and spent (i.e., realized) twice. It is good to know that the BTC successfully solves this double-spending problem through the blockchain concept with PoW, where each transaction is time-stamped.

A double-spending problem appears if two transactions (one of which is tricky) are sent into the network using the same private key (of a fraudulent money sender) to different receiving addresses. As these two transactions propagate through the network, one part of the network will accept one transaction and the other part, another. The defense mechanism inherent in the BTC blockchain is that only the transaction that miners first resolve into the next block (by any of two network parties) will be verified. The other one will be rejected as invalid. Such a confirmation mechanism through which the BTC manages the double-spending problem is enabled by a chronologically ordered, time-stamped transaction ledger, that is, by the blockchain.

The other breakthrough incorporated in the BTC is the use of PoW as a probabilistic solution to the class of failures known as the Byzantine Generals Problem [6], which is a generalized version of the Two Generals' Problem. It can be said that the BTC P2P network as a distributed system is Byzantine fault-tolerant (BFT).

The Byzantine Generals Problem can be presented, in a nutshell, through the situation in which more generals (each with his army) have to reach a consensus about the time of the attack in the forthcoming battle against the surrounded enemy. If they don't attack all together simultaneously, that is, if a few generals issue the order for attack and other generals do not, the enemy will overcome the armies that have attacked, gain strategic advantage, and eventually win the battle. Generals communicate to one another via messengers, that is, each general forwards a received message to the nearest few generals, depending on their spatial positions on terrain. The initial message with the information on the time of the attack is sent from the chief general to the few nearest generals and then relayed to the others. The problem occurs if some of the generals (the traitors) alter the received message and forward the messages with a different time of attack to other generals. This will lead to an unsynchronized attack and, eventually, to defeat in the battle. Since loyal generals do not know who the possible traitors are, they must create a communication protocol and the decision rules. These must ensure that, in a situation where some generals have received two or more messages with different times of attack, only the right message is accepted by all, and the false ones are rejected. It is shown [7] that this problem can only be solved if the number of traitorous generals does not exceed one-third of all generals.

When talking about the Byzantine Generals Problem in the context of distributed systems (such as the BTC P2P network), this problem concerns the corrupted components of the system having the symptoms that prevent other system's components from reaching an agreement among them (i.e., consensus). Such an agreement is needed for the correct operation of the system. Byzantine fault assumes any fault that causes a component to present different symptoms to different parts of the system. A Byzantine fault tolerance (BFT) system can accomplish its correct functioning if there are not too many faulty components, that is, if, at most, one-third of all components are faulty. BFT systems often include PoW as the mechanism to combat false pieces of information from corrupted components.

If we want to translate the Byzantine Generals Problem into a BTC environment, we can have a situation with a solved candidate block. Having found the solution, the miner adds the block to the blockchain (say, the n-th block) and broadcasts it to other nodes. Then, other nodes check the received blockchain with the added n-th block. Having done it and confirming the nonce, each miner adds this new block to the top of its copy of the blockchain. When the other miners continue adding the next solved blocks about every 10 min (i.e., blocks $n + 1$, $n + 2$, . . .) on top of block n, that block becomes solidified. The latest block on the top of the blockchain is usually unstable, but once there are more blocks on top of it, it is said to be more guaranteed. As each new block is difficult to add (because of PoW), a block within the blockchain is said to be secure after one hour approximately, that is, when six blocks are added after it. This is why most cryptocurrency exchanges and other services that accept Bitcoin usually wait for the so-called six blocks confirmation.

The last added block in the blockchain is considered unstable because it is quite possible (but not very often) that at that time, some other miner can find another solution and thus cause a fork in the blockchain. In this situation, the blockchain is split into two competing paths forward. Forks in a BTC blockchain appear regularly, and so far, each fork has been quickly resolved when an additional block was added to one of these two arms of the blockchain (which was lucky to be first prolonged). At the same time, the entire network abandons the block from the other arm (the orphan) since the winning arm contains more PoW. Hypothetically, if a fork remains unresolved, two competing blockchain histories would co-exist, compromising the whole system.

Theoretically, the Byzantine Generals Problem could appear if several miners or a mining pool do not follow the generally accepted rules when new blocks are added – namely, a very powerful attacker could try to troll the BTC community by adding enough hash power and outperforming the entire hash power of the network (the so-called "51% attack" [8]). One could try to impose their version of a blockchain, that is, initiate forking so that the last few (still unsolidified) blocks in the blockchain are replaced by some other blocks (in the new branch of the blockchain). These blocks might contain false transactions that nullify the transactions from the regular blockchain branch (causing double-spending) or corrupt the blockchain in another way. The attacker's version of the blockchain will be propagated through the network and accepted by the rest of the miners' community only if it contains more PoW than the regular version. This could happen only if the attacker owns a computing power sufficient to solve six consecutive blocks in a row (i.e., faster than the rest of miners). The probability of such an event in a given time becomes almost 100%, as the attacker's hash power comes closer to 50% of the total mining power [9]. In 2014, six blocks were solved in a row by the same mining pool, which concentrated more than 40% of the total hash power owned by the entire mining community. But then, some of the miners from that mining pool voluntarily moved to other pools trying to prevent unwanted effects.

An attacker might have significant hash power in a grey situation (somewhere between 30 and 50%), where there may be two or more different versions of a blockchain in the network. Consequently, it would lead to the crash of the BTC. But this will not happen due to the introduced PoW, which significantly reduces the probability of solving six consecutive blocks by the same entity. Besides, one may think that even with such a reduced probability, the attacker would have enough time to crash the system eventually. However, it is practically impossible, just due to the hash power added by the attacker. This is because, due to the increased overall computational power, the Difficulty of the involved PoW will also increase (after a maximum of two weeks). As a result, the attacker's hash power will still not be large enough to achieve his intention. So, it can be said that the BTC blockchain is a BFT system.

BTC's market value has reached several peaks so far. On the other hand, this increase in value motivated many attackers to try to hack or manipulate the BTC system, and a similar situation arose with a few other cryptocurrencies. Among many network-based types of attacks, two might disrupt the operation of the BTC network – partition attack and Delay Attack. Both attacks exploit some weaknesses of the Border Gateway Protocol (BGP) – not to confuse with the Byzantine Generals Problem – a broadly used routing protocol by the routers on the Internet.

These and other network-based attacks are possible since the BTC network is highly centralized, as seen from the Internet protocol routing perspective, – namely the three most significant Tier-1 Internet providers can intercept more than 60% of connections in the BTC network [10]. Apart from that, more than 60% of all BTC nodes are concentrated in five countries, led by the USA with around one-quarter of all nodes. On the other hand, mining power is concentrated in only one country – Chinese mining pools control approximately 80% of total hash power. The largest five mining pools are located in China, which mines approximately 70% of all new BTCs [11]. As a result, the centralization of mining power in a single country is one of the biggest issues for the BTC community, at the moment.

The precondition of a partition attack is the isolation of a group of victim nodes from the BTC network, where an attacker deliberately voids Internet traffic from/to the attacked nodes. In this way, the BTC network is split into two parts by the attacker (the smaller and the bigger), with no communication between them. Consequently, the block is solved in both network parts, and then each solved block is broadcast within its part. When the attacker stops the attack and establishes the communication between these parts again, all blocks mined within the smaller part (with less mining power) will be discarded, as will all the transactions and the miners' revenue.

The Delay Attack effectively slows down the propagation of blocks towards a victim. The main goal is to keep the victim node uninformed about a new block for almost 20 min. Unlike a partition attack where the victim's connection is voided, in a delay attack, the attacker conducts a Man-in-the-Middle attack between a victim and its peer node, modifying BTC messages sent from the victim. Due to the manipulation, a victim node (i.e., the miner) gets a different piece of information from the requested as the answer, that is, it gets what it did not ask for – that is, after mining a new block somewhere in the network, the new block's hash is announced and propagated through the network, reaching the victim node via its peer and via the attacker who intercepts the communication between the victim and its peer. Then, through the same channel (TCP connection with the peer node), the victim requests the solved block that matches the received hash. Nevertheless, the attacker alters this request to the peer (on behalf of the victim) by requesting the previously solved block that matches the other (i.e., the earlier) hash. After that, the victim's peer node sends the requested older block to the victim, and upon receipt, the victim ignores that block (as outdated) but still waits for the next 20 min to repeat the request. Eventually, the victim receives the right block from the same peer (while TCP connection with the peer is still alive). When the victim finally gets the asked block, it is too late then, as a new block is (most probably) solved and added to the blockchain. In this way, the victim wastes its computing power and time instead of solving the next block. The possible profit is lost as well.

Various measures can be used to combat or prevent both partition and Delay Attacks. They may include multi-homing [10] of a mining pool (to prevent Delay Attack), various filtering techniques applied by Internet service providers (against partition attack), BGP traffic monitoring, or upgrades of the BGP protocol (on appropriate routers) with security patches.

Numerous threats to different entities of the BTC system can also appear, which might cause problems if not treated properly. Without going into details, let us just name some of them: theft vulnerability of digital wallets, Sybil attack [12] (through creation of pseudo-identities of nodes), Denial of Service (DoS) attacks, energy consumption, tracing a coin's history (connecting identity with address), clock drift on a victim node (time jacking), illegal content in the blockchain, and so on.

1.2.3 Alternative platforms and cryptocurrencies based on blockchain

In the previous sections, the focus was on the BTC as the oldest and most prominent cryptocurrency. Besides, it served as a suitable example to explain the blockchain concept and mechanisms such as DL, PoW, community consensus, trustless truth, or incentive mechanism.

The success of the BTC paved the way for many alternate cryptocurrencies, known as altcoins. Among hundreds of altcoins, many are based on the same framework as the BTC, that is, they too include P2P network, blockchain, and a mining process with a kind of PoW to verify transactions on the web. On the other hand, altcoins differ among themselves and differ from the BTC in many ways – such as in PoW algorithms, procedural variations, different ways of spending energy for block mining, or the improvements taken for achieving better anonymity of users. After the BTC, the new alternate cryptocurrencies that emerged were created with the main goal of replacing the BTC, or, at least, repeat its success. Many altcoins are targeting the perceived constraints and shortcomings of the BTC and aim to achieve a few competitive advantages.

More than 1,500 altcoins have been created and launched on the Internet until now, and the new ones can show up at any time. However, many older cryptocurrencies are no longer present on the market. Currently, some of the altcoins with the largest market capitalizations are Ether (ETH), Cardano (ADA), Ripple (XRP), Litecoin (LTC), Zcash (ZEC), Dash (DASH), and Monero (XMR).

LTC, often mentioned as the silver to the BTC's gold, is very similar to the BTC in terms of functionality. The main differences are the average time needed for block solving of 150 s (four times shorter than the BTC's 10 min), the total amount of coins that can be mined (84 million LTCs compared to 21 million BTCs), and the applied PoW algorithm – LTC runs a script. This sequential function also involves SHA-256 [13] computations of hash but requires much more memory than the BTC's hash computations (known as double hash or hash-hash algorithm).

ETH is a bit more specific since it is not a digital currency – it, is not meant to be used for online payment of goods and services but as the incentive mechanism to power the Ethereum blockchain. In other words, ETH is the native digital currency (token) of the Ethereum network, based on which the Ethereum blockchain is designed for various decentralized applications using smart contracts (see Section 2). With the public Ethereum network's mining process, about every 12–15 s, a new block is verified, and the reward for this is 5 ETH. The PoW algorithm (called ethash) requires more memory than the one in the BTC. And also, for running various DApps, universal computing hardware is needed (like CPUs), so the expensive ASIC chips specialized in BTC mining, are not suitable for Ethereum mining.

The Ethereum DLT was the pioneer of the second generation of blockchain systems. Unlike the BTC, they are capable of smart contacts and decentralized applications. For a long time, Ethereum has been the only viable choice for DL platform selection for DApps. The possible alternatives were immature or had lacking DL ecosystems (see Section 2.7.1). The Ethereum technology is implemented in a large public network, with important crypto-market capitalization. In addition, the Ethereum ecosystem (see Section 2.7.1.1.) provides efficient community support, development tools, and libraries. Alternatives to PoW consensus have been supported in the Ethereum clients before, and one can use them in private or consortium networks. In 2021, the Ethereum Foundation also marked a clear migration path from the PoW consensus in the public network to the PoS. The Ethereum technology is, therefore, always an option for most advanced DApp designs. For the same reasons, many examples in this book refer to the Ethereum network, nodes, and applications.

Nevertheless, other viable DLTs and ecosystems are emerging. Some of them are presented in Section 2.7.1. They might differ from Ethereum in some of the approaches taken but share many of the common principles related to DL networks, performance, decentralized applications, and security, covered in Sections 2. and 3.

1.3 IOTA project – tangle

The Internet of Things (IoT) is becoming a reality with the expectation of deploying billions of IoT devices (shortly). Many of them are to be involved in different kinds of money transactions and micropayments. Therefore, there appeared a need for providing a universal platform that would support a huge number of transactions efficiently. This support should be much better than what the existing blockchain platforms can provide. A solution that should obtain key support to the IoT is offered by the IOTA project [14]. It is a new distributed ledger technology significantly different than the blockchain. IOTA is based on a specific DAG structure known as tangle.

The IOTA project began in 2015, intending to provide a more suitable cryptocurrency for payments (transactions) between billions of future IoT devices and obtain a reliable platform for many other applications, which might include M2M communication between those devices. As such, the implementation of the IOTA protocol had to be cheap, fast, and scalable, which was the key explanation for developing the tangle, instead of using already mature blockchain technology. The rapid growth of IoT significantly increased the demand for micropayments between IoT devices. At first, the BTC was seen to solve the needs of micropayments. However, it did not prove to be a good choice for two reasons. The first r is the relatively high fees as the amounts of money included in transactions reduce with micropayments, and the other reason is the roles of participants. – some miners verify transactions and "normal users" who issue transactions in the BTC society; hence, miners may be issuers, too. With this ambiguity, the probability of possible conflicts stays high, and conflict resolution wastes everyone's resources.

The key differences between IOTA and other blockchain-based systems such as the BTC or Ethereum are that IOTA's DLT includes no miners, no transaction blocks, no transaction fees or rewards paid in IOTA tokens, and no difficult PoW. Instead, when a participant broadcasts a transaction, the first thing to be done is to validate, that is, approve two (randomly chosen) previous transactions and perform a small amount of PoW. As a reward, the transaction is allowed to be attached to those two previous ones. After that, the attached transaction (called a tip) waits to be approved by a new transaction (of another participant), which then waits for its approval, later on. This pay-it-forward verification system makes financial rewards unnecessary.

Besides, the whole amount of the cryptocurrency (the IOTA tokens or IOTAs, in short) has already been created at the beginning of the tangle (i.e., at the genesis moment) and distributed to the project founders. After different transactions between participants (the founders and the new participants), IOTAs change hands. The smallest amount of IOTAs is one token (unlike the BTC, it is not divisible), while the total amount created in the genesis is $(3^{33}-1)/2 \approx 2.779 \times 10^{15}$ IOTAs.

As mentioned before, a tangle is a DAG, where each point represents an individual transaction (and not a transaction block), while arrows represent approvals. On a graph representing the tangle, each transaction points to the two previous transactions (the so-called parents) approved by that transaction (the so-called child). To clarify, the approvals (arrows on the graph) are in the opposite direction of the timeline's direction (Fig. 1.4). A transaction can be approved many times directly (by the transactions that directly point to it) or indirectly (by all further transactions that may indirectly point to it, following the arrows on the graph).

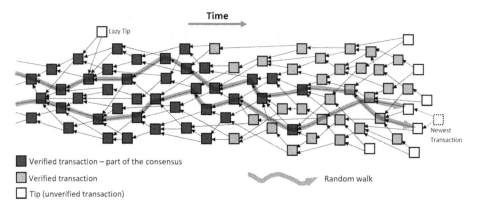

Fig. 1.4: Tangle – graph representation.

The first transaction in the tangle is called genesis. All IOTAs were created in the genesis, and there is no mechanism ever to create new ones. All transactions in the tangle approve the genesis directly or indirectly.

Having been approved by a large number of newer transactions, a transaction becomes a part of the consensus that is practically impossible to be changed. The consistency of a tangle is accomplished through a small PoW computation that has to be done by each transaction, making it too difficult for an attacker to fork or spam the tangle after consensus has been achieved. The consensus about a valid transaction is reached by applying the Random Walk Monte Carlo (RWMC) Algorithm [15]. This algorithm has to do with the way a new transaction selects two parent transactions to approve. The algorithm practically guides the transaction towards the tips (the not-approved transactions, yet) that have parents as young as possible. However, it is possible (but with a small probability) to select lazy tips, that is, tips that directly approve some older transactions (already verified by some earlier transactions in the past).

The mechanism of selection of a tip from the set of actual tips at the moment (in which it is also possible to be selected a lazy tip) is based on a random walk through the graph from the genesis towards the tangle's end (along the timeline), that is, towards the tips. When a particular tip is reached (i.e., selected), the walk stops. The walk is performed one more time, so that two tips are chosen first for validation. If the chosen tips are successfully validated (i.e., checked for inconsistency), they become parent transactions of the new transaction (which, practically, directly approves its parents). The cumulative weight of a transaction in the tangle is the total number of all transactions that came after, and at the same time, approved that transaction directly or indirectly (more precisely, this total number is additionally increased by 1). During the walk, at each branching point, the branch that will be chosen is the one that leads towards the next child transaction and that has the largest cumulative weight. Nevertheless, a certain amount of randomness will be introduced in the walk, that is, the transactions with the biggest cumulative weights at each branching point may not always be included in the path. It can be said that the walk is guided towards the heaviest branch. As new transactions come up, the tangle is forced to grow fastest in the directions that follow the paths with the heaviest transactions (in the sense of the cumulative weight). In contrast, the transactions appended to the lightest branches are orphaned, that is, it is most likely that they will never become a part of the consensus (since the probability of their approval by any new transaction is small). The growth of the tangle reminds one of the forced growth of a tree in one direction (e.g., where the tree receives the most light), while the growth in other directions is also possible but significantly reduced.

In the description given so far, the transactions in the tangle's interior are indirectly approved by all or by the majority of tips (~ 95% of tips). For that reason, they are considered confident and are expected to be present in the tangle forever, that is, there is a consensus on their immutability as parts of the ledger. The cumulative weight of a transaction is the measure of PoW performed after it, which secures the transaction's consistency and immutability in the same way that a block in a blockchain is secured and consolidated by PoW of later blocks. Larger cumulative weight of a transaction indicates that the transaction is more confident. When a transaction in the tangle reaches enough cumulative weight, it is safely included in the consensus. This is equivalent to the claim that the transaction becomes a part of the consensus if it is validated (mostly indirectly) by the majority of tips.

A common characteristic of blockchain-based systems and IOTA/tangle platform is that the IOTA network is also a P2P network of nodes (i.e., users, entities, and participants). But unlike, for instance, the BTC, nodes are entities, which, by design, both validate and issue transactions, since before issuing a transaction, a node must approve two earlier transactions issued by other nodes. Furthermore, each node is incentivized to remain active in propagating new transactions from other nodes through the network, although a node may not have other new transactions to issue. We need to avoid terminology confusion between nodes in the IOTA P2P network and sites in the tangle. A site is a transaction (issued by a node) in a tangle graph representation. Additionally, the tangle (as a representative of DLs) is the ledger for storing transactions that consist of a set of sites issued by nodes.

As for matters of timing, it can be said that the IOTA network is asynchronous, where a transaction may be issued at any moment by some node, and, after propagation through the network, it reaches different nodes at different time instances. This means that any other node, at the moment when it issues its transaction, does not operate with the actual state of a tangle but with the state from a few moments ago.

Consequently, a node, while running a tip selection algorithm, is unaware of the hidden tips that the node would be informed of shortly after that moment. Each node keeps (i.e., refreshes) its version of the tangle. In general, the versions on different nodes are not the same. Different nodes may see (more or less) different sets of transactions at any moment. However, these differences relate, at the most, to hidden tips, the newest tips, and recently verified transactions. In contrast, older transactions as a part of the consensus are common (i.e., the same) for a great majority of nodes.

A node does not always necessarily contain the latest version of the ledger or continuously forwards received updates (the new received tips) to its neighbors (peers) in the network. It is quite possible that when a node has a new transaction to issue, it can choose to verify two parent transactions from an older state of the tangle (when the node may work offline and is not always connected to the Internet). After verification, the node broadcasts its new transaction (which is appended to the verified parent transactions) through the network. The node does not help the community as it does not approve any new transaction.

On the other hand, such lazy behavior is punished by the protocol in two ways. Firstly, the issued transaction will probably be considered by the remaining part of the network as a lazy tip, because other active nodes have fresher versions of the tangle. Since the lazy tips will be most probably orphaned, it is unlikely that such transactions will ever become a part of the consensus. Nodes are motivated to maintain their ledger versions as fresh as possible. Secondly, nodes are directly motivated to share new transactions from other nodes, as they increase the probability of verifying their recently issued transactions in that way. When verified, they also increase their cumulative weights, which enlarge the chances of becoming part of the consensus, finally. However even in a case when a node has no transactions for issuing, it is incentivized to propagate transactions from other nodes. According to the protocol, the mechanism that forces nodes to propagate transactions is that every node calculates the statistics about the number of new transactions received from each peer. If a node does not share new transactions, it will be dropped by its peers. So, next time the node has a transaction to issue, it will not be able do it.

With the above-described incentive mechanisms, which do not include any transaction fee, the tangle is getting cheap – one of the desired features in IoT applications (which is not the case with Ethereum and other blockchains). Tangle is seen as a good IoT support, as it is also fast and scalable. Unlike blockchain, tangle does not assume transaction blocks, so the number of transactions per second is measured in thousands, that is, it is much higher than in a BTC blockchain. And also, the tangle is scalable by design, since the more transactions are created, the more transactions are validated and confirmed.

The participants issuing transactions also contribute to the tangle's security through resolving possible conflicts – namely, during the verification of two parent transactions, a node checks if the verified transactions are conflicting. A transaction may be conflicting with some other transaction (i.e., with the tangle history) in different ways. For example, an entity (a person or an IoT device) purchasing some goods or service and sending IOTA tokens to the other entity (seller) in a transaction, may have a negative account balance calculated from all previous transactions in the tangle (beginning from the genesis event). The negative balance can be a result of conflict between earlier transactions. Also, even with a positive account state, a dishonest entity might spend its money twice by issuing two different transactions to different sellers in a short period (double-spending problem), resulting in two conflicting transactions. As there is no conflict prevention mechanism, the tangle may contain pairs of conflicting transactions for a while.

When a node selects two tips for its child transaction to be appended to them, it has to validate those tips first. The validation of a tip includes checking the tip's signature and its PoW, as well as making sure that the tip is not in conflict with any of the transactions in its validation path, that is, with the transactions which are directly and indirectly referenced (i.e., validated) by this tip. Suppose the node finds that the selected tip conflicts. The node leaves that tip and chooses another one, while the previously selected tip is forgotten. In that way, a node resolves conflicts directly. The same happens if the node finds a conflict between any two transactions in the validation path of the selected tip. In that case, the conflict is said to have been resolved indirectly. If a node issues a new transaction that indirectly approves conflicting transactions, it risks that other nodes will not approve its new transaction.

Another situation in which the tangle performs self-purification through resolving conflicts is when a node selects two tips where the validation path of the first tip contains a transaction that conflicts with a transaction in the validation path of the second selected tip. This is when none of the two transactions in the conflict belongs to the intersection of validation paths of these two tips. In such a case, the node does not see the conflict. Therefore, both of the two conflicting transactions are indirectly approved by the node by appending its transaction to the selected tips. Furthermore, a few new transactions might be appended to it without seeing the conflict.

Nevertheless, a new transaction will select a tip with the validation path containing both conflicted transactions sooner or later. Then, the conflict will be registered and resolved by abandoning that tip. That tip will be orphaned together with several previous transactions that the tip has directly or indirectly validated. These orphaned transactions will include only one of the conflicting transactions (and a few subsequent transactions which have approved it). In contrast, the branch that contains the second conflicting transaction (the one with a higher cumulative weight) will survive. Hence, the conflict is resolved, and only one of the two conflicting transactions stays in the ledger. Several innocent transactions, which have approved the other conflicting transaction (because they had not been in a position to detect the conflict), will be orphaned as collateral damage. However, most probably, they will be picked up and reissued by the participants (nodes) involved in these transactions as sellers (payment recipients).

As already pointed out, a tangle began in the genesis event, where the very first transaction started distributing a predefined total amount of IOTA tokens. As the tangle grows and the total number of transactions increases, the size of the ledger is continually getting bigger, which may be a problem, especially for IoT applications. To reduce the size of a tangle, the IOTA Foundation makes snapshots of the full network from time to time. A snapshot contains states on the accounts of all users (wallets' balances), but it does not contain transaction history, that is, all previous transactions are erased. Such a snapshot represents a new genesis state of a tangle (like a new beginning), but with the difference that the total amount of 2.779×1015 tokens has already been distributed to all existing users at that moment.

Currently, the IOTA network is not fully developed, and the number of users is far beyond the number for which the tangle was initially designed. As a result, the community's total computing power (hash rate) is still relatively low. Consequently, the current tangle is vulnerable to double-spending attacks, which would be possible if an attacker owned more than one-third of the total network hash rate. To prevent attacks of this kind and for security reasons, IOTA users apply (voluntarily and temporarily) a different consensus mechanism through the so-called Coordinator. This mechanism assumes that the IOTA Foundation issues a milestone transaction every two minutes. All transactions approved directly or indirectly by a milestone transaction are immediately considered part of consensus (i.e., with the confirmation confidence of 100%). In the future, when the IOTA network reaches a large enough computing power, the Coordinator will not be necessary, that is, IOTA Foundation will shut it down and let the tangle evolve entirely on its own.

A special characteristic of the tangle is that all processing and software calculations are run in ternary logic, or more precisely, in the balanced ternary logic. Unlike binary computing, where a binary digit (bit) can take one of two values (0 and 1), a digit in a balanced ternary, called Tritt, can be –1, 0, or + 1. A word of three Tritts is called Tryte (analogously to byte), and it can have $3^3 = 27$ different states (values). Each of Tryte states is designated in IOTA with one of the 26 uppercase letters "A", "B", "C", . . ., "X", "Y", "Z" and the number "9" as a symbol (symbol "9" in balanced ternary logic represents value + 1).

Computer theory defines a measure for the efficiency of a hypothetical computer with the radix (base) R, called radix economy, as the product of R and the number of digits in that base. Theoretically, base $e = 2.71$ (Euler's number, i.e., the base of natural logarithm) would be maximally efficient in storing information. Still, for a real computer, radix $R = 3$ is the best choice, since this is the integer closest to e. Furthermore, balanced ternary has an advantage over positive ternary (also called vanilla ternary, where digits can have values 0, 1, and 2) in allowing the encoding of positive and negative numbers in the same way. There is no such thing as the binary representation of negative numbers in the 2's complement, so no-sign Tritt is needed. Also, there are other advantages, for example, simpler truth tables for digit addition, subtraction, multiplication, and division.

The rationale for involving ternary computing in IOTA is also based on research in this area, whereby ternary and quantum computing are seen as the near future. Ternary computers (except a few experimental ones) do not exist. Therefore, the whole ternary logic (including computing of cryptographic hash function, like SHA-3) is emulated and run by conventional binary computers in IOTA.

1.3.1 IOTA bundle

As we have already previously explained, a new transaction's first step is to select two tips (using the random walk) that are to be approved by that transaction. And yet, the real implementation is a bit more complicated since, most commonly, a common transaction is issued through the so-called bundle of several individual transactions (Fig. 1.5), where each transaction has the same value as its internal field named Bundle Hash. In other words, for each real transfer of IOTAs from one participant to another, the appropriate software client issues not only one transaction but a chain of N individual transactions related to that transfer (which are indexed in reversed order from $N - 1$ to 0). All transactions in a bundle together approve the two selected tips according to a specific scheme (this will be explained in the following chapters).

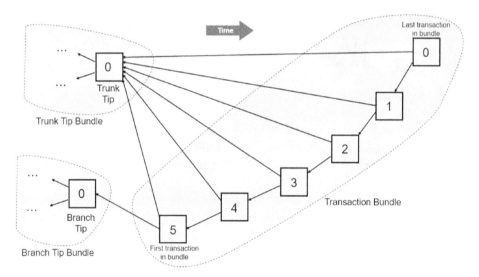

Fig. 1.5: Transactions bundling in a tangle – an example of a bundle with six transactions.

The selected tip chosen after the first random walk is called the trunk tip. The other tip, which is chosen after the second random walk, is called the branch tip. The first individual transaction in the bundle (with index $N - 1$) approves, that is, points to both trunk and branch tip, while the remaining $N - 1$ individual transactions (with indices from $N - 2$ to 0) all together point to the trunk tip. Each of these $N - 1$ transactions, besides the trunk tip, also approves the previous transaction in the bundle (with the index higher by 1) through the internal field Trunk Transaction (which contains the hash value of the previous transaction in the bundle), see Fig. 1.6. This means that the value written in the Trunk Transaction field is equal to the value written in the Transaction Hash field of the previous transaction in the bundle. In contrast, the value of the Branch Transaction field is equal to the hash of the trunk tip (written in the Transaction Hash field of the trunk tip). As already explained, the first transaction in the bundle approves both selected tips, but in a slightly different way – its Trunk Transaction field now points to the trunk tip, and the Branch Transaction field points to the branch tip.

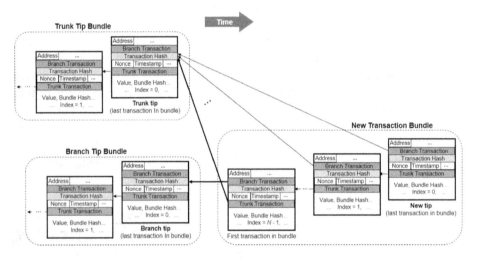

Fig. 1.6: Way of transactions bundling in a tangle.

In the end, each tip belongs to its bundle as the last (not approved) individual transaction of the bundle, since the random walk algorithm selects only those not-yet-approved transactions (each of the earlier transactions in a bundle is already approved by the last one, i.e., by the tip).

There are three types of individual transactions in an IOTA bundle: input, output, and meta transaction. The type of a transaction depends on the sign of the number written in the internal field, Value, representing the amount of IOTA tokens (IOTAs) that are to be added (through this individual transaction) to the account specified by the field, Address. As a result, the content of the field, Value, in an input transaction is a negative number, which means that the given address is charged for the specified amount of IOTAs. An output transaction adds IOTAs to the given address since the written value is positive, while a Meta transaction is neutral as the value written in it equals 0. Meta transactions are used as extensions of input transactions, usually having the tail parts of the input transactions' signatures.

Let us explain it with the following example: if client A wants to make a purchase and transfer, for example, 700 IOTAs to client B, the client software on A's side will create a bundle of input, output, and (probably) meta transactions which are to be integrated into the tangle. Thereby, either all transactions inside the bundle will be accepted by the nodes in the IOTA network or none of them. In the process of bundle creation, at first, the output transaction containing the address b of client B in the Address field and the positive value of 700 in the Value field is prepared. This transaction gets assigned index 0 (this transaction is indexed as the beginning of the bundle of N transactions, but it will be issued last in time, in the burst of N bundled transactions).

Next, the input and meta transactions are prepared. If client A has, for example, three addresses (i.e., three accounts) a_1, a_2, and a_3 generated from the same private keys seed, with the account states of 200, 600, and 350 IOTAs on them, respectively, the three corresponding input transactions will have the following values written in the Index, Address and Value fields: $\{1, a_1, -200\}$, $\{3, a_2, -600\}$ and $\{5, a_3, -350\}$. Since input transactions need to contain transaction signatures where the address security level is two by default, a meta transaction is added after each input transaction to carry the second part of the signature of the preceding input transaction. These three meta transactions will have the following indices, addresses, and values: $\{2, a_1, 0\}$, $\{4, a_2, 0\}$ and $\{6, a_3, 0\}$.

An output transaction is prepared as the last one to balance the transfer (the so-called remaining transaction). Since client A spent $200 + 600 + 350 = 1{,}150$ tokens through the three input transactions, and client B received 700 tokens through the first output transaction, a new output transaction is created, which returns the difference of $1{,}150 - 700 = 450$ tokens to client A. This transaction has index 7 (the biggest in the bundle), value 450 (positive), and address a_4 (created from the same seed as the addresses a_1, a_2, and a_3 of client A).

In the end, the complete bundle in a given example contains eight individual transactions with the following {"Index", "Address", "Value"} triplets: $\{0, b, 700\}$, $\{1, a_1, -200\}$, $\{2, a_1, 0\}$, $\{3, a_2, -600\}$, $\{4, a_2, 0\}$, $\{5, a_3, -350\}$, $\{6, a_3, 0\}$, and $\{7, a_4, 450\}$. The first and last transactions in this example are of the output type, while the transactions in the middle are of input or meta-type. In general, the total number of transactions in a bundle is not limited, but practically, under given network constraints and limitations of the PoW difficulty, the issuance of bundles with over 30 transactions is discouraged. A typical bundle for a transfer between two clients (sender and receiver of tokens) consists of four transactions: one output (to receiving client), one input (from sender), one meta-transaction, and the balancing transaction.

1.4 Hashgraph

Led by the BTC development so far, blockchain technology has made a significant breakthrough in the DL area and has opened up the opportunity for creating numerous decentralized applications, apart from cryptocurrency (which is only one of them, but the most popular one). Several DL systems based on DAGs have also emerged, aiming to develop new technologies with the best possible and most desirable features. However, these features are often in opposition to one another. Hence, the existing systems such as BTC, Ethereum, or IOTA/Tangle are just the trade-offs based on the level of their realization. An ideal DLT should certainly have the following properties: immutability, low latency, security, scalability, low computing difficulty, DDoS resistance, as well as modesty in Internet bandwidth requirements. It is also important that such a system should not require any expensive server. It should be fair, fast, cheap, and Byzantine fault-tolerant. Finally, it should have the ability to achieve a consensus under circumstances of the absolute trustless truth, that is, enforce the community's rules, even when nobody trusts anyone. A good candidate that fulfills all these requirements is a DL platform known as hashgraph.

Hashgraph [3] is a new DAG-based consensus alternative to the blockchain. Simply put, a DAG is a finite directed graph without loops between any two elements. In graph theory, a graph is a structure consisting of a set of points (vertices, elements, squares) where any two points can be in relation, that is, connected by a line (edge, arc). A directed graph means that each line between two points is directed, that is, has an arrow. Thus, a DAG can be considered to be a finite set of points connected by arrows, so that there is no way to start at any point X and follow a sequence of arrows that eventually loops back to X again, that is, that there are no directed cycles. A DAG can have a tree topology (as a special case), but generally, DAGs have no regular topology. Blockchain could be considered as the simplest DAG with the points (blocks) connected in a chain, that is, one where each point (except the first and the last one) has one predecessor (parent) and one successor (child).

There are similarities between graph representations of hashgraph and IOTA/tangle: both have topologies of a DAG where each element (event, i.e., site) has exactly two direct ancestors (parents). However, this is their only similarity. It can be concluded that the DAG of a hashgraph represents the history of all communications (the so-called gossips) between a community (population) members.

Hashgraph runs a gossip protocol, which, in brief, can be described as follows: in the hashgraph's P2P network of nodes, at any moment, every node, X (member of the population, participant) can synchronize with its randomly chosen neighbor, Y (peer), where X sends a sync message to Y, containing information about new transaction(s), about previous sync messages (gossips) between nodes in the population, or both. Thereby, node X sends everything it knows so far and what node Y does not know, that is, X sends everything to Y, except the pieces of information that X is sure that Y has already learned.

When a node receives a sync message, it creates a data structure called an event. In general, an event contains (as payload) a set of the most recent transactions learned from the node's clients, that is, from users (digital wallets), and the timestamp representing the moment at which the node claims to have received the sync. A sync message from node X to node Y consists of all the events known to X and unknown to Y (i.e., for which X supposes that they are unknown to Y). On the other hand, node Y extracts only (to its own) unknown events until that moment (since Y may have already learned some of the received events from other nodes' syncs, which node X was unaware of). Node Y uses the new information to update its copy of the hashgraph ledger as the overall picture of all events and syncs in the population, from the beginning.

In the graph representation, for example, when a node A receives a gossip (sync) from a node B, that gossip event is shown on the graph as a circle (vertex) in column A, with two lines (edges) going down to the immediately preceding gossip events by nodes A and B (Fig. 1.7). The hashgraph diagram (such as the one in Fig. 1.7c) is used only for its presentation and explanation, that is, there is no actual graph stored in memory anywhere.

For sharing of transactions, each node runs two endless parallel program loops in its software. It asynchronously receives and collects new transactions from its clients (wallets) and the sync messages from other nodes (thereby creating events) in the first loop. In the second program loop, the node occasionally sends syncs to its neighbor nodes. This process of gossip spreading, that is, sharing the existing and creating the new events, should stop when each node collects every piece of information (on all transactions) created or received at the beginning, that is, when a consensus about all transactions and about the timeline of their occurrences is reached. However, as new transactions appear all the time, the process practically never stops, since there is always something new to gossip about. At the same time, nodes are continuously reaching the consensus on the previous events and fast. Practically, at any moment, every node can see almost the same picture (i.e., the history) of all events as the other nodes are seeing. In contrast, the differences (between nodes' views on overall gossip history) are only related to the latest events (which may be old a few seconds, maximally).

Knowing that sync messages include information not only on the events' transactions but information on the events per se, as well, it can be said that hashgraph represents gossip about transactions, as well as gossip about gossip. This is important because, from the history of gossips, a node can conclude which information other nodes know and which they do not.

Let us conclude, in short, that hashgraph is a hybrid data structure – the combination of a hash and a graph, which keeps records about who gossiped to whom and in what order. Hashgraph does not require any PoW (so there is no mining), since reaching the consensus relies on a procedure known as virtual voting. Unlike blockchain, where transaction data is stored in blocks, hashgraph stores data in events, so an event can be comprehended as a container of transactions, although an event may be empty. In the hashgraph, an event and all the transactions contained in it almost immediately become part of a permanent record, that is, of the copy of a ledger on every node. This is performed as soon as the node gossips that event and all other nodes hear about it. Also, in only a few seconds, every node will know, with 100% certainty, about the event's position in the hashgraph's history, and every node will know that every other node knows this (which is of even greater importance).

Furthermore, unlike the BTC blockchain, where a block and the whole PoW invested in its solving might be sometimes wasted (e.g., in the case of a blockchain forking, when two candidate blocks are solved at about the same time, after which only one block survives), with hashgraph, no event is ever sacrificed, so hashgraph's efficiency is 100%, as well. Finally, hashgraph is a Byzantine fault-tolerant system, where the BFT property is absolute, that is, mathematically proven (the case will be discussed later).

Figure 1.7a shows the beginning of a hashgraph for the population with five members (participants, nodes) in the network, named from A to E. Over time, as new events are created, the hashgraph grows upwards. Grey circles at the bottom of Fig. 1.7a represent events created by each member, at the start. Every new event created by a member will be added above the last event on the vertical line that belongs to that member.

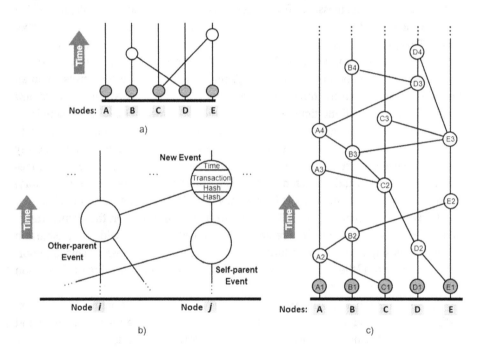

Fig. 1.7: Structure of hashgraph.

An event is a small data structure, which can contain zero or more transactions. Every event has two parent events below it (except the start events): one, which is called self-parent, and the other one, which is called other-parent. A vertical line connects an event and its self-parent event (they are in the same column since the same node creates both), while an angled line connects the event with its other-parent event (earlier created by another node). Besides the field for transactions (if they exist), there are three more fields in the data structure of an event: two fields containing hashes of two parent events and the field for the timestamp of the event's creation (Fig. 1.7b).

A node that has created an event also signs it digitally. When the node gossips that event to another node, the signature is sent together with the gossiped event(s). The whole hashgraph structure is firmly bonded and protected, that is, made cryptographically immutable, since each event contains hashes of its parents – that is, after each received sync message and creating a new event, a node can pass through the hashgraph from the starting (or from some later) event/s and calculate by itself, the hashes of the events below the other parent, as well as the other parent's hash. In that way, the node can check the correctness of the other-parent event (and the events below) and validate it, which it certainly does. After sync is received, only validated events are included in the node's copy of the hashgraph. Furthermore, nodes in the hashgraph's P2P network communicate to each other using TLS encryption protocol (on top of TCP), which additionally protects the exchange of sync messages.

Figure 1.7c shows an example of a hashgraph (with five nodes/participants) for the first few events, where it can be seen who gossiped which events to whom and in what order. For example, participant (node) C first gossips (sends sync) event C1 to participant A which, upon the receipt of C1, creates event A2. Node A saves events C1 and A2 in its file system and the transactions that might be contained in them. Event A2 as payload contains only new transactions (if any collected in the meantime) with the timestamp of the event's creation and the hashes of its parents A1 and C1 as overhead. Then, participant E gossips event E1 to D, after which participant D creates event D2. In the next step, A synchronizes with B, so A gossips everything he knows (events A1 and C1) to B, who then creates event B2. The gossip from Fig. 1.7c is then spread as follows:

SYNC (B→E): B gossips events B2, B1, A2, A1, and C1; node E creates event E2
SYNC (D→C): D gossips events D2, D1, and E1; node C creates event C2
SYNC (C→A): C gossips events C2, D2, D1, and E1 (C does not send C1 since C knows that A has already learned of C1 in the previous C→A sync); node A creates event A3
SYNC (C→B): C gossips events C2, C1, D2, D1, and E1 (at that moment, C does not know that B has already learned of C1 in A→B sync, since node C is yet unaware of that sync, so the event C1 was not excluded from this gossip); from this moment, node B knows of all starting events A1–E1; node B creates event B3
SYNC (B→E): B gossips events B3, C2, D2, and D1 (now, B knows that E has learned of B2, B1, A2, A1, and C1, so these events are not gossiped about, neither is E1, since it was created by E); from this moment, node E knows of all starting events A1–E1; node E creates event E3
SYNC (B→A): B gossips events B2, B1, C2, D2, D1, and E1 (at that moment, B does not know that A has learned of C2, so C2 was not excluded from the gossip; on the other hand, B knows that A knows of C1, so C1 is not

sent); from this moment node, C knows of all starting events A1–E1; node A creates event A4

SYNC (E→C): E gossips events E2, B3, B2, B1, A2, and A1 (now E sees C2 via B3. Hence, E knows that C knows of D2, D1, and E1, so these events are not gossiped about); from this moment, node C knows of all starting events A1–E1; node C creates event C3

SYNC (A→D): A gossips events A4, A3, A2, A1, B3, B2, B1, C2, and C1; finally, from this moment, node D knows of all starting events A1–E1; node D creates event D3

This process occurs very fast, so every node in the community learns of all starting events (A1–E1) and their transactions in a very short time (~ a second). The same also applies to any new transaction/event that appears later. At every moment, all nodes reach a full consensus on the transactions' and events' existence from the start and up to very close to the actual moment. However, for hashgraph applications (cryptocurrency, smart contracts, file storage), to be resistant to double-spending, Byzantine Generals Problem, Sybil attacks, and other types of misuses, this kind of consensus is not enough. The community must also achieve the consensus on the exact order in time of all events, and for that purpose, the virtual voting consensus algorithm is used.

Virtual voting is a voting process in which the community of nodes collectively and democratically establishes the consensus on the transactions' order in time, that is, on the transactions' timestamps. It is called virtual because nodes do not send their votes over the Internet (the Yes/No decisions regarding famous witnesses, which will be explained later). Instead, each node calculates what votes other nodes would have sent, based on its knowledge of what other nodes know. Each transaction's timestamp adopted by consensus represents the moment when the majority (more than 50%) of the network members (nodes) learned of that transaction. The consensus timestamp of a transaction is determined as the median value in a set of timestamps that pick the moments when each node says that it, for the first time, received an event (through gossip) having this transaction. In other words, timestamps written in events created upon each node's first reception of gossip with the given transaction are seen as elements of the set of timestamps, whereby the set's median value is declared as the transaction's consensus timestamp.

And yet, every node is not allowed by default to delegate its event, that is, the event's timestamp to be an element of the mentioned set of timestamps. To get this allowance, each node must create, a bit later, an event that is elected as the famous witness, that is, as the event, which the hashgraph shows that most nodes have learned of, fairly soon after it was created. Generally speaking, virtual voting is the Byzantine agreement mechanism that determines which nodes may delegate (and which may not) the timestamps for calculation of the events' median (i.e., consensus) timestamps.

In a population of members (nodes), any group that gathers more than two-thirds of the total number of nodes represents the so-called supermajority (while for a simple majority, only more than 50% of nodes are needed). The term supermajority can also refer to events, that is, to the witnesses of a round (explained below), in which case, it represents a group that counts at least 2/3 of witnesses.

If, in a hashgraph diagram, there is at least one path between any two events X and Y, that connects them directly or via other events (e.g., assuming that X is older than Y), it is said that Y sees X and that event X is an ancestor of event Y, that is, Y is a descendant of X. If X and Y are linked via only one path, which includes events Z and W, it is said that Y sees X through Z and W. In general, Y can see X via more paths and each path can include more events, whereby different paths may partly overlap (i.e., may have common events). The union of all events belonging to all paths between X and Y represents the set of events through which Y sees X. If the supermajority of nodes creates such a set of events, it is said that Y strongly sees X.

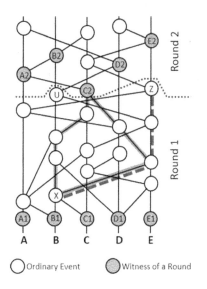

- C2 sees X via two paths (grey), 4 nodes involved (B, C, D, E) which is supermajority (since 4/5 > 2/3) → **C2 sees X strongly**
- Z sees X via one path (dashed), 2 nodes involved (B, E) which is not supermajority (since 2/5 < 2/3) → **Z doesn't see X strongly**
- U sees the following witnesses of Round 1:
  A1, through 4 nodes (A, B, C, E) → U sees A1 strongly
  B1, through 4 nodes (A, B, C, E) → U sees B1 strongly
  C1, through 3 nodes (B, C, E) → U doesn't see C1 strongly
  D1, through 3 nodes (B, D, E) → U doesn't see D1 strongly
  E1, through 3 nodes (B, C, E) → U doesn't see E1 strongly
  U doesn't see strongly any supermajority of Round 1 witnesses → **U stays in Round 1** (not a witness of Round 2; U has round created of 1)
- C2 sees strongly: A1 (through A, B, C, E), B1 (through A, B, C, D, E), C1 (through B, C, D, E) and D1 (through B, C, D, E);
  C2 sees E1 (through C, D, E), but not strongly
  C2 sees a supermajority of Round 1 witnesses → **C2 is the first witness of Round 2** (C2 has round created of 2)
- Z sees strongly: C1 (through A, C, D, E), D1 (through A, C, D, E) and E1 (through A, C, D, E); Z also sees A1 (through A, C, E) and B1 (through A, B, E) but not strongly → Z doesn't see strongly any supermajority of Round 1; **Z has round created of 1** (although appeared after C2); Z is not a witness of Round 2
- D2 sees strongly: A1 (through A, B, C, D, E), B1 (through A, B, C, D, E), C1 (through B, C, D, E), D1 (through B, C, D, E) and E1 (through B, C, D, E)
  D2 sees strongly all Round 1 witnesses → **D2 is also a witness of Round 2** (D2 has round created of 2)...

Fig. 1.8: Example of seeing strongly and illustration of division on rounds.

The hashgraph is divided into the portions of events called rounds (see Fig. 1.8). It starts with round 1, and the starting events (from each node) are called witnesses of round 1. As the hashgraph grows, an event will appear at one moment, which strongly sees a supermajority of the round 1 witnesses. Round 2 begins from that moment, while this event becomes a witness of round 2. The division of rounds is based on a rule that each next round begins with the first event, which strongly sees a supermajority of the witnesses in the last round (the event does not have to see all the witnesses from the last round). This event becomes the first witness of the next round. Each node may have created at most one witness in a round implying that some nodes may have created no witness in the round. Also, when an event is first gossiped to a node, that node can immediately calculate the round created of the event, that is, the serial number of the round the event belongs to. The round created of an event is calculated as follows: if the event sees strongly a supermajority of witnesses of round r, where r is the max of the round created of the event's parents, then the round created of the event is $r + 1$; otherwise, the round created of the event is r.

The following step is used to determine which of the witnesses in a given round will be (virtually) elected as the famous witnesses. Every witness in a round can become famous if some conditions are satisfied. Whether the i-th witness, $W_{n,i}$ from round n will be famous or not is up to the witnesses from upper rounds, $n + 1$ and $n + 2$ (in most cases). Firstly, each witness, $W_{n+1,j}$ from round $n + 1$ gives his virtual vote, that is, answers "Yes" if he can see $W_{n,i}$ (strongly seeing is not mandatory here) or the answer "No" in the opposite case. Next, these votes are counted by witnesses from round $n + 2$.

As a result of this, a witness, $W_{n+2,k}$ from round $n + 2$ takes into account (i.e., collects) only the votes from round $n + 1$ witnesses, which he strongly sees. The votes from other round $n + 1$ witnesses, not strongly seen by $W_{n+2,k}$ (if any of them exist), are not considered. If the number of collected "Yes" votes is greater than or equal to 2/3 of the total number of nodes (a supermajority), then it is decided that witness, $W_{n,i}$ is famous.

The same virtual voting procedure is performed for each round n witnesses, so eventually a group of the famous witnesses of round n will be formed, the fame of which was finally decided by only one witness from round $n + 2$, that is by a witness who counted the votes of round $n + 1$ witnesses. It was mathematically proven that the same result of the election of the round n famous witnesses would be obtained if any other round $n + 2$ witness counts the votes of round $n + 1$ witnesses.

The nodes that have created famous witnesses of round n are given the allowance to make decisions on consensus timestamps of some events (i.e., transactions) from round $n - 1$. More precisely said, the creator nodes of the round n famous witnesses are qualified to determine the consensus timestamps of the events from round $n - 1$, which are seen by all famous witnesses of round n. If an event is seen by all the round n famous witnesses, this event is said to be received (by the community of nodes) in round n, that is, that it has round received of n. For example, to determine the consensus timestamp of a round $n - 1$ event, X_{n-1} which has round received of n, each node A_i from this privileged group (of the creators of the round n famous witnesses) first picks the event, Y_i, which was created by that node when it first received a gossip with given event, X_{n-1} (it may often happen that Y_i is just the famous witness of round n, created by that node). In the next phase, the timestamp of event Y_i is delegated as one of the candidates for the consensus timestamp of event, X_{n-1}. Lastly, the candidate timestamps delegated by all qualified (i.e., privileged) nodes are sorted into an array of timestamps beginning from the oldest one, and the timestamp in the middle (the median value) is declared as the consensus timestamp of event, X_{n-1}. In case there are two middle timestamps in the array (i.e., when the number of candidates is even), the latter is chosen.

Getting the timestamp consensus (see Fig. 1.9) of event X_{n-1} is repeated for every event from round $n - 1$ having round received of n, while other round $n - 1$ events wait to be seen by all famous witnesses from round $n + 1$ (or higher). As the hashgraph grows with time, the consensus timestamps of the events, which belong to rounds n, $n + 1$, $n + 2$, . . . (having round received of $n + 1$, $n + 2$, $n + 3$ . . . respectively) are determined by following the same virtual voting procedure on the upper

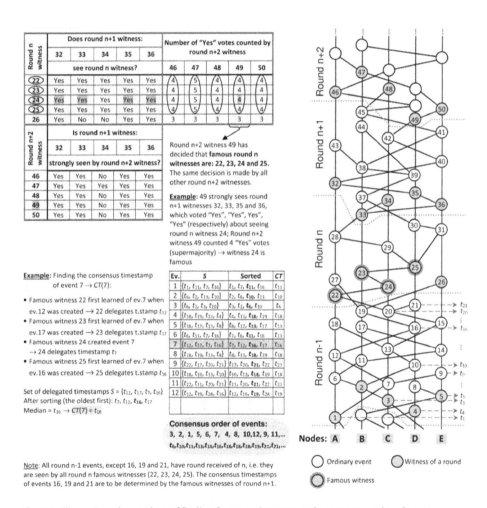

Round n witness	Does round n+1 witness:					Number of "Yes" votes counted by round n+2 witness				
	32	33	34	35	36	46	47	48	49	50
	see round n witness?									
22	Yes	Yes	Yes	Yes	Yes	4	5	4	4	4
23	Yes	Yes	Yes	Yes	Yes	4	5	4	4	4
24	Yes	Yes	Yes	Yes	Yes	4	5	4	4	4
25	Yes	Yes	Yes	Yes	Yes	4	5	4	4	4
26	Yes	No	No	Yes	Yes	3	3	3	3	3

Round n+2 witness	Is round n+1 witness:				
	32	33	34	35	36
	strongly seen by round n+2 witness?				
46	Yes	Yes	No	Yes	Yes
47	Yes	Yes	Yes	Yes	Yes
48	Yes	Yes	No	Yes	Yes
49	Yes	Yes	No	Yes	Yes
50	Yes	Yes	No	Yes	Yes

Round n+2 witness 49 has decided that famous round n witnesses are: 22, 23, 24 and 25. The same decision is made by all other round n+2 witnesses.

Example: 49 strongly sees round n+1 witnesses 32, 33, 35 and 36, which voted "Yes", "Yes", Yes", "Yes" (respectively) about seeing round n witness 24; Round n+2 witness 49 counted 4 "Yes" votes (supermajority) → witness 24 is famous

Example: Finding the consensus timestamp of event 7 → CT(7):

- Famous witness 22 first learned of ev.7 when ev.12 was created → 22 delegates t.stamp t_{12}
- Famous witness 23 first learned of ev.7 when ev.17 was created → 23 delegates t.stamp t_{17}
- Famous witness 24 created event 7 → 24 delegates timestamp t_7
- Famous witness 25 first learned of ev.7 when ev.16 was created → 25 delegates t.stamp t_{16}

Set of delegated timestamps $S = \{t_{12}, t_{17}, t_7, t_{16}\}$
After sorting (the oldest first): $t_7, t_{12}, t_{16}, t_{17}$
Median $= t_{16}$ → $CT(7) = t_{16}$

Ev.	S	Sorted	CT
1	$\{t_1, t_{11}, t_7, t_{16}\}$	t_1, t_7, t_{11}, t_{16}	t_{11}
2	$\{t_6, t_2, t_{13}, t_{10}\}$	t_2, t_6, t_{10}, t_{13}	t_{10}
3	$\{t_6, t_2, t_3, t_{10}\}$	t_3, t_2, t_6, t_{10}	t_6
4	$\{t_{18}, t_{19}, t_{13}, t_4\}$	$t_4, t_{13}, t_{18}, t_{19}$	t_{18}
5	$\{t_{18}, t_{17}, t_{13}, t_8\}$	$t_8, t_{13}, t_{13}, t_{17}$	t_{13}
6	$\{t_6, t_{11}, t_7, t_{16}\}$	t_7, t_6, t_{11}, t_{16}	t_{13}
7	$\{t_{12}, t_{17}, t_7, t_{16}\}$	$t_7, t_{12}, t_{16}, t_{17}$	t_{16}
8	$\{t_{18}, t_{19}, t_{13}, t_8\}$	$t_8, t_{13}, t_{18}, t_{19}$	t_{18}
9	$\{t_{22}, t_{17}, t_{20}, t_{21}\}$	$t_{17}, t_{20}, t_{21}, t_{22}$	t_{21}
10	$\{t_{18}, t_{19}, t_{13}, t_{10}\}$	$t_{10}, t_{13}, t_{18}, t_{19}$	t_{18}
11	$\{t_{22}, t_{11}, t_{20}, t_{23}\}$	$t_{11}, t_{20}, t_{21}, t_{22}$	t_{21}
12	$\{t_{12}, t_{19}, t_{24}, t_{16}\}$	$t_{12}, t_{16}, t_{19}, t_{24}$	t_{19}

Consensus order of events:
3, 2, 1, 5, 6, 7, 4, 8, 10,12, 9, 11,...
$t_6, t_{10}, t_{11}, t_{13}, t_{13}, t_{16}, t_{18}, t_{18}, t_{18}, t_{19}, t_{21}, t_{21},...$

Nodes: A B C D E

○ Ordinary event   ◎ Witness of a round   ⬤ Famous witness

<u>Note</u>: All round n-1 events, except 16, 19 and 21, have round received of n, i.e. they are seen by all round n famous witnesses (22, 23, 24, 25). The consensus timestamps of events 16, 19 and 21 are to be determined by the famous witnesses of round n+1.

Fig. 1.9: Illustration of procedure of finding famous witnesses and consensus order of events.

rounds' witnesses. In this way, the consensus timestamps of events (and of the transactions contained) begin being determined after practically two rounds, that is, in only a few seconds after the given event's creation. The consensus on the existence of an event is achieved even faster. Of course, the virtual voting process may encounter ties regarding the election of the round n famous witnesses. The witnesses from round $n + 3$ (and even from higher rounds) are engaged in resolving the voting ties. This certainly prolongs the time of reaching the timestamp consensus, that is, the consensus on the time order of the round $n - 1$ events, but, even then, the whole process is very fast.

After determining consensus timestamps of all events in a round, the consensus on their time order is automatically achieved, which was the aim of the whole procedure. The consensus timestamps of events are assigned to the transactions they contain, so the consensus on the order of transactions is determined too. The consensus timestamp of a transaction is fair, since it reflects the moment when the majority of nodes received that transaction, as this timestamp cannot be corrupted or significantly changed by a malicious node. In case some malicious nodes try to delay or stop a transaction and thus exclude it from gossips, the transaction will bypass that obstacle due to the random nature of the gossip protocol.

The whole idea of splitting into rounds, elections of famous witnesses, etc., might seem too complicated. But this is not an issue, since the software that implements the hashgraph on a node does not require any special hardware – it requires nothing more than an average computer with a CPU for universal purposes. It does require an Internet connection with the bandwidth necessary for downloading and uploading a given number of transactions per second and exchanging syncs with other nodes in the hashgraph's P2P network. Thus, the amount of gossiped data between two nodes is minimal. As mentioned earlier, within a sync message, a node sends only the events it supposes to be unknown to its peer/neighbor node. Moreover, some events are sent without hashes of the events' parents (when sending node can conclude that the receiving node can calculate those hashes). Besides, the hashgraph's virtual voting algorithm does not require any additional bandwidth. As a reference to be noted, a fast home Internet connection (of each node) would be fast enough to support the same number of transactions per second as the entire VISA card network can handle worldwide. Another indicator of the hashgraph's speed is the test results for the network of 32 computers (nodes) spread across eight regions around the globe. Namely, when this network runs at 50,000 transactions per second, the consensus on the time order of transactions is reached in 3 s. If the whole network is concentrated in a single region, the time needed for consensus is 0.75 s. Also, the same number of computers (spread in eight regions worldwide) can provide the performances required by credit cards – the latency of fewer than 7 s to handle up to 200,000 transactions per second.

There are other advantages of the described concept of virtual voting. The most important one is the hashgraph's BFT property, achieved in the strict sense of the BFT definition (and mathematically proven), unlike blockchain or tangle technologies where BFT is accomplished only as a possibility. To be specific, the hashgraph's honest members will be able to keep running a given application (e.g., cryptocurrency) correctly, even where the number of fraudulent members/nodes is very close to 1/3 of the whole population. The BFT property of a hashgraph is a direct consequence of the implemented rules (i.e., of the Byzantine protocols) within virtual voting. The strongly seeing and the supermajorities of nodes and witnesses are required.

The second advantage is that all voting processes and getting consensus time-stamps are performed virtually and independently by each node. Every member/node does everything on its own, as if it was alone on a desert island and without the need for any additional communication with anyone (except the regular gossip). Besides a reduced demand for Internet bandwidth, the benefit of this is also an increased speed of realization and verification of transactions. To be specific, an alternative consensus algorithm that would obtain BFT property certainly should be running separate Byzantine protocols, including a large amount of communication between all members. Thus, if the aim is to determine the consensus order of all events in time, each separate communication between two nodes would contain several Yes/No questions (in both directions), where each question would have the form, "did event X come before event Y?" However, such an algorithm would be very slow due to the delays in communication between nodes over the Internet, and perhaps due to its complexity.

Instead of all mentioned so far, by applying the virtual voting algorithm, the Byzantine agreement protocol is run only for witnesses, whereby famous witnesses are chosen as a result of a small number of questions, such as: "Is this witness famous?" In this way, the process of time event ordering (through performing some sorting algorithm) is avoided. As already explained, the time order of events is (automatically) determined as soon as their consensus timestamps are found, as the median values of the candidate timestamps delegated by the nodes that have created the famous witnesses.

In the previous paragraphs, some of the factors for realizing an application based on hashgraph are that it should be fast, cheap, Byzantine fault-tolerant, resistant to double-spending and DDoS attacks, and modest in the bandwidth demands. Other desirable features of hashgraph are related to its organizational structure designed to make these features real. For the time being, Hashgraph is a project in its developing phase. It is led by Hedera Hashgraph, LLC – the company which also provides a public ledger platform for this project. It was mentioned earlier that a DL could be permissionless or permissioned, depending on whether a central entity grants the permissions to nodes for accessing the network or not. Also, it was mentioned that a DL network could be private or public based on the P2P network used. The Hedera hashgraph platform is designed to be public and to have permissionless (i.e., open) consensus with a permissioned (closed) governance.

The closed governance model is based on the idea that the platform will be governed by a council of up to 39 reputable organizations and enterprises from different industries and regions worldwide, with highly respected brands. The Hedera

Hashgraph Council (HHC) is a governing body aiming at supporting the evolution of a stable and decentralized public ledger infrastructure based on the hashgraph consensus algorithm. HHC will follow the rules to ensure that no single member or a small group of members will have control over the body as a whole. On behalf of the council, the elected Governing Board will establish the council membership policy, then regulate the network rules and token issuance, and approve changes to the platform codebase. The governance rules foster the philosophy of decentralization and prevent the concentration of power over the process of reaching the consensus on the transaction order in the platform. Such a governing model will also eliminate the risk of ledger splitting, guarantee the codebase integrity, and provide open access to the protected core. Protected core means that the hashgraph consensus algorithm is not license-free. Specifically, the intellectual property rights in the algorithm are held by Swirlds, Inc. (the company founded by the inventors of the algorithm). At the same time, the HHC has a license from Swirlds to use it for the Hedera public DL platform. On the other hand, neither license nor Hedera's approval will be required to use the Hedera hashgraph platform or write software that uses the platform services. In contrast, the applications built upon the platform can be open source or proprietary.

Properties necessary for the broad adoption of a DL platform are trust and stability. Hedera's governance model (with its governing rules) and the implemented strong security mechanisms are just the key factors for a stable decentralized platform that creates trust. Apart from that, the HHC's policies and structure are intended to guarantee a wide and fair distribution of native cryptocurrency of the Hedera DL platform and to ensure a full network nodes' application. As a result, the nodes will be compensated for the services in maintaining the Hashgraph platform through the specially designed incentive model. And consequently, at the same time, the new nodes (i.e., new node operators) will be able to join the network.

The entire system of payments (incentives) and fees introduced by Hedera significantly differs from the incentive mechanism of the BTC (or other altcoins), where the clients (i.e., digital wallets) pay a fee for each verified transaction. At the same time, nodes earn money through mining if they are successful in solving the PoW tasks. As explained, the Hashgraph is not based on PoW, so there is no mining that would motivate nodes to perform transaction verification. Instead, Hedera hashgraph's paying model is based on three types of fees to nodes or to Hedera paid by clients, and on two types of payments which Hedera pays to nodes or governing members:

- Node fee – a client pays this fee to a node for a provided service. Suppose the client wants to transfer cryptocurrency from his to another's account. In that case, he contacts a node that submits the transaction to the network (on the client's behalf), that is, the node puts that transaction into the next event it creates and gossips it to a neighbor node to be put into consensus through the hashgraph consensus mechanism. Node fee is not determined in advance, but it is negotiated between node and client.

- Service fee – a client pays this fee to Hedera for the service provided by the plat-form. The fee is calculated based on the service provided (transaction, file stor-age, or smart contract) and the quantity of the service (e.g., in the case of file storage, the service fee depends on the number and sizes of stored files).
- Network fee – with this fee, a client compensates the node for the network costs, that is, for the cost of gossiping the client's transaction, the cost of temporarily storing the transaction in memory, and the cost of calculating the timestamp con-sensus of the event containing the transaction. The fee for each transaction has a fixed part and a variable part, which depends on the number of bytes in the trans-action. The network fee is paid to the node, but then, it is forwarded to Hedera.
- Incentive payment – to incentivize nodes to maintain the Hashgraph, Hedera makes payments to nodes once a day. This money is taken from the amount that Hedera collects from the service and network fees. The amount paid to a node is proportional to the stake the node owns, but to be paid, the node must be online and active the whole day (e.g., it may be that during 24-h period, the node con-tributes with a minimum of one event each, to at least 90% of rounds)
- Dividend payments – Hedera may make these payments periodically to the gov-erning members as a reward for their role in governance.

Through the combination of open (permissionless) consensus and closed (permis-sioned) governance, the Hedera hashgraph platform aims to build more public trust than an entirely closed system, which is the key factor for a cryptocurrency to achieve global acceptance. The open consensus model assumes a process where nodes join the network and (in the way explained earlier) reach the transaction timestamp con-sensus, that is, the consensus in the time order of transactions. In order to ensure transparency, this process enables the possibility of anonymous individuals joining the network as node operators. On the other hand, it opens the door for various mis-uses of the Hashgraph. These include Sybil attacks or the cases of the concentration of power over consensus by a few dishonest members, who could use their power to, for instance, modify the ledger inappropriately, counterfeit the cryptocurrency, or in-fluence the consensus order of transactions, among others. Nevertheless, these threats are prevented by designing a consensus model that encourages the emergence of a decentralized network with many thousands of nodes. Weighting votes inhibit the conspiracies of groups of nodes and Sybil attacks in the hashgraph virtual voting algorithm.

The virtual voting algorithm described earlier in this section assumed that the votes of all relevant nodes in the hashgraph were equal. Hedera introduced a modi-fication in the algorithm to eliminate collisions – the weighting of nodes' votes based on the nodes' stakes. In other words, each node casts one vote for each coin (of Hedera native cryptocurrency) the node owns, so the influence of a node on the consensus process is proportional to the amount of cryptocurrency in the node's possession. This type of consensus is known as the Proof of Stake (PoS), the idea of which is explained in Section 1. When a node joins the network, it must declare accounts that it can control, while the amount of cryptocurrency in those accounts is used as the stake that weights the node's votes in the hashgraph virtual voting algorithm. As mentioned, each node is paid by Hedera on a daily basis (for serving as a node) – the payments are proportional to its stake, so the stake of a node is effectively earning interest.

The vote weighting in the virtual voting algorithm is relatively easy to implement – it can be done through a simple redefinition of the notions of the majority, supermajority, and the median value. Instead of at least 2/3 of the number of nodes in the community, the term supermajority now represents a group of nodes whose stakes in the sum have at least 2/3 of the total amount of money on the accounts of all nodes in the community. Similarly, the term majority is redefined, and it now means more than 50% of the total amount of stakes. The median of the timestamps in a set S of the events' timestamps now becomes the weighted median, which can be considered as the median value of the new enlarged set, $S_{enlarged}$ of the timestamps, where each timestamp t_i from S is, in $S_{enlarged}$, represented by n_i identical copies of itself, assuming that n_i is equal to the stake of the node that has created the event with timestamp t_i.

The new meaning of supermajority implicitly changes the definition of strong seeing of events in the Hashgraph. Together with the new meaning of the median (i.e., weighted median), it influences the order of the consensus transactions, so that the wealthier (hence, the more trusted) nodes have more power to reach the consensus than some group of new nodes with insincere intentions.

Besides the described mechanisms incorporated in the Hashgraph, such as the fee and payment model aimed at incentivizing node operators to participate, or the PoS model for inhibition of Sybil attacks and other malicious behaviors, Hedera introduces the so-called sharding architecture to ensure future scalability of the platform, which is also necessary for the success of a public permissionless ledger. This architecture comes from the separation of governance from consensus. As the network is expected to expand over time to millions of nodes (all voting on distributed consensus), the sharding architecture enables continuous platform decentralization.

In its initial phase, the Hedera network will certainly have a relatively small number of nodes belonging to a single shard (partition, group). With the expected increase of their number in the network, nodes will randomly be grouped in different shards. The entity in charge of allocating nodes to shards is called the master shard, which randomly assigns new nodes to different shards, once a day. At the same time, the master shard moves some nodes between shards to ensure that the total amount of cryptocurrency staked in a shard is large enough and that no node in a shard owns a large fraction of that amount. All nodes in a shard establish consensus on the transactions they collected from their clients and gossiped among themselves, that is, they share the same state of their client's accounts, which is a subset of the state of the entire ledger.

Shards are not mutually isolated – occasionally, any member in a shard can send a message to a randomly chosen member in some other shard. Each shard maintains outgoing message queues for all other shards. Suppose client, C_a of node A in the shard α wants to send some amount of cryptocurrency to client, C_b of node B in the shard β. This transaction is first gossiped by node A to the nodes in the shard α. After reaching the consensus on the order in the shard α, the account state of client, C_a is decreased by the amount being sent.

An inter-shard message is also created and put in the outgoing queue for the shard β. Subsequently, at one moment, some node, X, from the shard α will check that queue and, seeing that it is not empty, X will send this inter-shard message (which contains transaction $C_a{\rightarrow}C_b$) together with other messages (with other transactions from the shard α to β, if any) to a randomly chosen node, Y, in the shard β. When Y receives that list of messages, it creates an event containing all the transactions from the received messages and submits this event to the nodes in the shard β through gossip. When a transaction, $C_a{\rightarrow}C_b$ reaches consensus in the shard β (and if the sequence number of the assigned inter-shard message is correct), the effect of the transaction will be applied on all nodes in β, and the account balance of C_b will be increased by the amount being sent.

The positive effects of the sharding architecture can be seen from the above described (and simplified) example of the communication between shards in a situation when the number of nodes in the network is very large. The number of gossips between nodes in the entire network would be many times greater without it, consensus and transactions delay would be much longer, and the nodes' ledger files would be much bigger. The separation on shards minimizes the total amount of gossip messages in the network, since each transaction is gossiped only within shards relevant for that transaction.

The Hedera hashgraph platform comprises three layers: the Internet layer, hashgraph consensus layer, and service layer. The Internet layer provides a basic communication infrastructure for the nodes, that is, for the computers connected to a P2P network, communicating by TCP/IP connections with applied TLS encryption. The hashgraph consensus layer represents the described process in which nodes take transactions from their clients. They share them throughout the network using gossip protocol and run the hashgraph consensus algorithm to reach the consensus in time transaction order. Then, each node applies the transactions' effects in consensus order, that is, modifies its copy of the shared state (of the clients' accounts), which is identical with the copies on all other nodes of a given shard.

A service layer provides three initial services, relying on the two lower layers:
- Cryptocurrency
- File storage
- Smart contracts

By offering these services, Hedera intends to realize the idea similar to one of the Ethereum networks, where its native cryptocurrency (ETH) is primarily used as the incentive tool to power the Ethereum blockchain, primarily designed to support different decentralized applications (e.g., in the form of smart contracts). Hedera also uses its native cryptocurrency to incentivize nodes (to serve as nodes) through its payment model. However, unlike Ethereum, this is not the only (i.e., primary) role of the Hedera cryptocurrency, as the service of processing transactions between clients is also important. The developers of decentralized applications on the Hedera platform will use its initial services and pay for them in Hedera tokens (native cryptocurrency) through the service fees. The Hedera cryptocurrency is expected to have a high transaction rate as well, due to the very fast hashgraph consensus algorithm. This leads to low network fees, making small, micro transactions practical. Therefore, the Hedera cryptocurrency should be suitable for IoT applications, too.

Hedera tokens are also used as the means of weighting the virtual voting mechanism within Hedera's staking model – as mentioned. In contrast, PoS contributes to network security, for example, to inhibit Sybil attacks. On that aspect, tokens should act as the motivating factor for the responsible use and governance of the Hedera platform. The total amount of cryptocurrency that Hedera plans to issue is 50 billion tokens; thus, the token release schedule will be very slow in the beginning. In the first year, the expected distribution of tokens is that about 65% of the total amount will be held by Hedera Treasury and the rest by trusted nodes, that is, the nodes hosted by Hedera management, employees, investors, developers, and Swirlds, Inc. Thus, only 10% of the total amount should be circulating among clients through transactions, and this amount is expected to increase slowly. To be specific, the amount of circulating tokens should not exceed the threshold of 33% for at least five years from the initial release. The goal of these precautions is to prevent situations in which an attacker (or group of attackers), who owns one-third of the tokens, could disrupt the network (since in the Hedera's PoS model, a transaction becomes final when validated by the nodes that hold at least two-thirds of tokens in the sum).

Using the second initial service of Hedera – the file storage, users will be able to store decentralized files or pointers to files on the Hedera hashgraph platform, reliably and transparently. This means that the copy of each added file is stored on every node with 100% availability and with the consensus on the exact content of the file. The consensus is reached in the same way as for transactions, that is, by using a hashgraph consensus algorithm. The concerning events in the hashgraph now contain another type of data (instead of transactions). As every node in a shard holds an identical copy of the file, it will not be lost if one or a few more nodes are corrupted or out of service. A stored file can be deleted from the platform only by the entities with a given consent. Decentralized applications could use this service to realize different types of registers (such as land ownership registers, property title registers, movable asset registries, etc.).

The third initial service of Hedera – smart contracts, is enabled through the possibility of containing short computer programs (i.e., code) instead of transactions within hashgraph's events. The execution of these programs, which are written in Solidity programming language, is guaranteed on all (honest) nodes as soon as the consensus on the events is reached. It is done in the same way the effects of a transaction are guaranteed to be applied to the account states of the relevant clients on each node's copy of the ledger, at the moment when the community validates the transaction and reaches the timestamp consensus on that transaction. The smart contract service allows developers to easily build a broad spectrum of decentralized applications on top of the Hedera platform. Smart contracts practically open up the possibility of signing the contracts between people, organizations, entities, and so on, where it is guaranteed (with 100% confidence) that each clause of a signed contract will be executed precisely and at the exact moment as has been agreed (i.e., written in the program code). Currently, large libraries of the code written in Solidity can be run on the Hedera platform (although the Solidity programming language was initially developed to execute smart contracts on Ethereum's platform). More about smart contracts and decentralized applications are covered in Section 2.4.

It is clear now that hashgraph technology comprises all the characteristics needed to overcome today's gap between cryptocurrency and the real world. The hashgraph's inventors aimed to create a part of the current cyberspace that can be shared among members, who have agreed to act upon the predefined rules. This space will be independent, with no negative effects on the members (based on monopoly) or the security issues that big technology companies may have, hosting large amounts of confidential data. During the testing phase, there will be a small number of nodes within the Hedera network, after which the trusted nodes (all run by the HHC members) will join the network. In the next phase, other participants will be gradually included until the moment of allowed membership to anyone ready to host the node, provided they meet the necessary technical requirements of bandwidth, computing power, and storage. In the final stage, the Hedera network is expected to have millions of nodes worldwide and that many of them will be run by ordinary people who want to stay anonymous.

2 Decentralized applications

Decentralized applications (DApps) are application paradigms that combine on-chain application logic executed in the DL network with traditional application engineering approaches. The DL network assures trusted execution of the on-chain logic (i.e., smart contracts) while Web, mobile, server-side, or embedded applications provide user and machine interfaces for the DApps.

DL networks differ in the applied technologies, as also in their organization and governance. These factors jointly contribute to the trust, performance, and scalability of a DL network. Smart contracts and off-chain applications adopt some of the known software engineering approaches. At the same time, a decentralized environment and immutable ledgers require certain adaptations.

Apart from the key services provided by a DL network, DL ecosystems often accommodate additional distributed and support services, too. These services facilitate, for example, bulk decentralized and distributed storage, a combination of smart contracts and off-chain data sources, user-friendly naming of decentralized resources, or monitoring of a running DL network.

Decentralized application architects and developers rely on DL technologies and support services. However, for DApps productization, they require business-grade development and support ecosystems and third-party services in order to focus on application development. Productization of decentralized applications is a significant step towards broader adoption of these, still relatively novel, technologies and solutions.

2.1 Decentralized trust - distribution vs. decentralization

Two related characteristics are required and contribute to decentralized trust in distributed ledger systems. These are:
- The distributed nature of ledgers
- Their decentralized control

Let us consider a simple database system that is installed on a computer. It is united/consolidated in a single instance and is thus not distributed. The system control is centralized in the hands of the system proprietor, who manages access rights for all the system users. Note that the proprietors can appoint another user to manage the system on their behalf. However, even in this case, they keep the right to override any of the users' actions and still fully control the system. For performance or other reasons, the database system can be scaled over several computers. A distributed system topology enables many essential benefits, including redundancy, eliminating single points of failure, resilience to failures, or performance scalability. Modern cloud and network virtualization systems allow the highly efficient and scalable distribution of

https://doi.org/10.1515/9783110681130-002

systems. However, the control of the entire system would remain centralized with the proprietor, and the access policies would remain very similar to the one in the consolidated implementation.

To disperse the administration (governance) of the system so that there is no single entity having control over the system, we need a different approach, that is, decentralization of control. Such a system has to be distributed as many instances are building the system. Unlike in the distributed and centralized database example, each instance is controlled by a different entity in a decentralized system. These can be, for example, users who install and run blockchain nodes or consortium partners who agree to commonly run a DL network and, therefore, all set up their node instances. De/centralization in DLs is, thus, more organizational in nature and not technical. However, the underlying technology has to provide a distributed system, which is a prerequisite for its decentralized governance. The actions in the system cannot be based on an arbitrary decision of a single proprietor but are based on a mutual consensus. The same consensus mechanism is implemented in every node instance. These mechanisms assure that all the actions can be conducted only in the pre-agreed way, even if some of the system participants act maliciously.

A DL system is distributed, by nature. If, in addition, we implement it in a way that facilitates decentralized governance, we get a decentralized trusted system. Unlike in centralized trusted systems, where we need to trust the system proprietor (e.g., a bank, holding a database with client account and balance information), in decentralized trusted systems, there is no central entity we would have to trust. The trust is assured by DL protocols, which are commonly open source and, hence, available for verification to anyone.

Table 2.1 shows that a consolidated topology, where the governance can only be centralized, provides only centralized trust. In distributed systems with centralized governance, no decentralized trust can be assured either. Only those systems, which are distributed and decentralized, can provide decentralized trust.

Tab. 2.1: Decentralized trust: relations between topology and governance of a communication system.

		Governance	
		Decentralized	**Centralized**
Topology	Consolidated	Not applicable	Centralized trust
	Distributed	Decentralized trust	Centralized trust

The decentralized trust in DLs is the fundament for the trusted exchange of transactions among system participants. Transactions are validated and immutably and non-refutably stored in a ledger as a part of a new chain block or a related data structure in other ledger architectures (see Section 1 for details). Trusted exchange of transactions is essential for cryptocurrencies and, hence, the immense proliferation of distributed ledger technology. However, modern DL platforms, apart from the trusted exchange of transactions, also enable trusted execution of programming code–smart contracts. Smart contracts are one of the key elements of decentralized applications, discussed in Section 2.4.

2.2 DApp triplet

The term decentralized application is not precisely defined. Despite being present for more than a decade now, DLs and blockchains are still evolving concepts and technologies, so terminology, too, is maturing along with the research, practical developments, new DL-based application domains, and use cases. In this book, we refer to DApps [16] as decentralized software systems with three components. We call these three components, the DApp triplet (see Fig. 2.1):

- A decentralized overlay distributed ledger network for trusted exchange of transactions
- The on-chain application logic that is executed in a trusted way in the overlay network
- The off-chain application logic implemented outside of the overlay network that can utilize both the trusted exchange of transactions and the trusted execution of the on-chain application logic

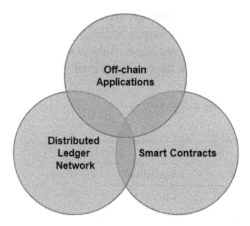

Fig. 2.1: DApp triplet: DL network, smart contracts, and off-chain applications.

At a very high level, DApp architecture can be compared to modern Web applications, which comprise backend and frontend, and require a communication network that interconnects the two. In the backend, the application logic that requires, for example, big data storage or complex computations is usually implemented. The frontend part of the application is oriented more towards the client user interfaces or logic in the embedded systems in IoT. Backend exposes an application programming interface (API), for example REST API, to exchange JSON structured content between backend and frontend. Communication connectivity is assured via the Internet protocol (IP) networks.

In DApps, the backend is assured by the smart contracts, the application logic running on the DL network. It is therefore called the on-chain logic/application part, too. Frontend applications in DApp are Web, mobile, or embedded applications. They do not run on the DL network (thus the off-chain application part) but access the backend services through the APIs exposed by the DL network nodes.

2.3 DL networks

A DL network is an incarnation of a particular DL technology. The DL technology (DLT) is implemented in a network node, and interconnected nodes build the network. There can be many different networks based on the same DLT. Figure 2.2 shows that the DL operation is a set of application layer protocols that resides on a traditional TCP/IP stack and builds an overlay network. Similar communication topology is found in, for example, peer-to-peer (P2P) content distribution systems. For example, some of the communication principles in Ethereum have been directly adopted from the existing P2P systems. Unlike in the client-server communication topology, there are no central entities in a distributed DL network. All the nodes/clients have equal roles in providing communication capabilities. Peer nodes make the topology resilient and scalable. A node is thus a piece of software. Other denominations for a node are possible, too. A DL node is frequently referred to as a client. A node runs the DL protocols such as:
- Low-level P2P network protocols for node discovery, network formation, flow control, or encryption of the traffic
- High-level P2P communication protocols for node identity, session management, and data exchange between the nodes
- Upper layer protocols for exchanging data for synchronizing the chain among the nodes, for example, block headers, and for exchanging transactions
- Protocols for building transactions, including hashing and message serialization
- Consensus protocols for mining nodes
- Various node, network management, and service utilization protocols and APIs

Based on the scope of activated capabilities, the nodes in a DL network can be divided roughly into three categories:
- The full nodes: each node keeps a copy of the entire ledger and synchronizes it continuously. These nodes are essential for the distribution of the network. They assure the validity of the ledger and the security of the DL system. Maintaining a

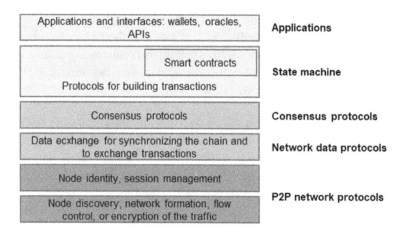

Fig. 2.2: DL network reference model.

copy of the entire ledger (every block, every transaction, and all the meta-data for the ledger structure) might result in extensive storage requirements.

- The light nodes: do not keep a copy of the entire ledger. They may have just the last part of it or partial information, e.g., block headers but not the block content. Light nodes impose modest system requirements and enable faster ledger synchronization, if the nodes' connectivity is intermittent.
- The mining nodes: can be full or light nodes. Their key characteristic is running the ledger consensus protocols (see Section 1 and 1.2.1 for more details) to participate in the ledger building process. Mining is not a mandatory function of every DL node. However, it is frequently implemented in the standard node software and can be arbitrarily enabled.
- The access nodes: can be full or light nodes. They expose APIs for off-chain applications to interact with the DL network (see Section 2.5.2 for more details). As in mining, exposing the API is not a mandatory function, either.

But our interest in DL networks reaches beyond the technical aspects. It also includes the network governance, performance, and all the settings, tweaks, and new developments to adapt the DLTs for new, challenging use cases.

2.3.1 Network organization and governance

Network governance covers various elements of the control of network nodes and, in this way, the control over the entire network and its services. The governance is as important as the DL technology for two essential qualities of DL networks:

- Performance
- Security or trust

In the governance of the network operation and the use of its services, two aspects need to be distinguished:
- Control of the network nodes and, thus, the control of the consensus process
- User access to the network services, for example, creating accounts, transactions, or transferring funds to another account.

In a DL network, the governance approaches for the two aspects need not be the same. For example, network services might be available freely without special access control. In contrast, in the same network, the management of the existing nodes and installation of additional mining nodes might strictly be limited to the network proprietor only. This might cause a wrong impression in uninformed users about the network's actual levels of trust and security. If the network control is centralized, we can trust the network only if we fully trust the network proprietor (just as in a traditional database example, given in Section 2.1). No (un)restricted service access or claims about network distribution can eliminate the need for trust in a central entity. A valid question, in this case, would be: "*Do we really need a DL in this case?*"

2.3.1.1 Public, private, and consortium networks

Section 2.1 clarified that the distribution of entities in a DL network is the prerequisite for decentralized trust. A distributed system can be decentralized or not. The approach to decentralization in the network defines the level of trust one can have in such a network. Well-known public blockchain networks such as the Bitcoin and Ethereum networks (see Section 1.2) are highly distributed. At the same time, they impose no limitations on who can add new nodes to the network, create accounts and transactions, or participate in the mining process. Hence, they are decentralized, too.

For illustration, there were an estimated 7,000-8,000 nodes in public Ethereum mainnet in 2021 [17, 18] and about 10,000 publicly listed full nodes in the Bitcoin network [19]. It is difficult to estimate the number of miners, as they are mainly organized into mining pools. Besides, to participate in mining, a node does not have to be a full node, and most miners are not. Another estimate states that around 100,000 separate mining nodes in Bitcoin were organized in mining pools in 2021. A similar number was reported for the Ethereum mainnet, too.

A public DL network relies solely on the high level of decentralization and implemented security algorithms to ensure the consensus among the honest majority of nodes. This provides security to the network and excludes malicious nodes from the network. In public DL networks, both the network control and service access are unrestricted. Such a network is a prerequisite to set up trusted decentralized cryptocurrencies, which was the first motivation of many of the DLTs. There are many prominent examples of public DL networks, for example, Bitcoin and Ethereum.

A private DL network is distributed, but the governance of the nodes and network is centralized to a single system proprietor. It, therefore, does not provide any decentralized trust. Limited or unlimited user service access cannot compensate for this lack of decentralization. Sometimes, the privately controlled networks tend to be presented as being public, primarily to gain the trust in the cryptocurrencies they provide. In the current version 1.0 of the IOTA network, for example, they only become genuinely valid when the network Coordinator node confirms them. All Coordinator nodes are operated and controlled by the IOTA Foundation, which has, in the past, already utilized this to modify the transaction ledger.

In a private DL network, we can apply the same technology and even the same initial setting as a public network. For example, we can use the same network node software (e.g., the Geth client for Ethereum), select the same consensus algorithm, and apply the same chain genesis settings as in the private Ethereum mainnet. We would probably have a much lower number of nodes in our network, but the operation of both networks would be very similar. There would be, of course, a difference in the chain data, but this would be due to different service usage patterns and not different network operations. The key difference between the public and or private network would thus be in their governance, apart from the use, of course.

Nevertheless, in private DL networks, we usually do not try to mimic the existent public ones. Instead, we apply different chain genesis settings or even changed DL protocols to improve network performance, vastly. The key benefit of a private DL network is that we can trim it for performance.

The challenge of centralized governance in public networks can, to a large extent, be limited in the consortium DL networks. Here, the network control is still not public, but it is also not limited to a single central entity. Usually, a consortium of partners is built, having a common objective – for example, a DApp that interconnects distributed energy resource prosumers, who do not necessarily trust each other but are interested in collaboration. Every consortium partner can set up nodes and participate in consensus decisions, so the control is now, to some extent, decentralized. It is still not as decentralized as in the public networks, but this might even not be needed. In a consortium network, we do not have anonymous participants in the network, so the outlaw can be penalized in other ways, for example, with exclusion from the partnership or with legal measures. Consortium-based DL network governance is widespread in financial or IoT business applications. Some of the prominent public DL networks have consortium-based network control and not a pubic one, as, for example, the Hedera public network (see Section 2.7.1.3 for details).

2.3.1.2 Permissioned and permissionless networks

The public or private nature of a DL network is based on the mode of network access. It can be:
- Permissioned
- Permissionless

In public networks, access to the network services is permissionless. This means that a new network user (usually a person) does not have to possess any dedicated rights to create new accounts, build and submit transactions, or even add new nodes to the network, including mining nodes. The participant thus remains anonymous and is identified only by his randomly created DL network addresses. The relation between the real users and their DL addresses does not have to be disclosed to participate in the network or utilize its services.

In a permissioned system, users are authorized to access the network services or participate in the network control. There are several benefits of permissioning in DL. Permissioned network control can enable better network performance and is easier to be managed. A permissioned network also does not require a cryptocurrency to incentivize the mining process, which positively affects transaction costs. All these benefits of permissioned network control reflect in the network services provided to the user. Besides, permissioned DL systems can facilitate compliance with regulations like GPRD.

The terms public and permissionless are often seen as synonymous. The public is then understood as having no formal identity (vs. permissioned, with identity). This might be true for many of the public DL networks, including Bitcoin and Ethereum. Nevertheless, a private or consortium-controlled network might provide permissionless public network services, too (Fig. 2.3). Operation of the network and user access to network services are two distinct aspects of network governance and do not have to apply different governance and permission principles. Thus, some of the DLT taxonomies

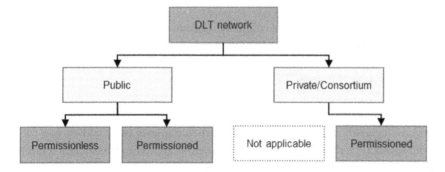

Fig. 2.3: DL network taxonomy.

[20] discuss public-permissioned systems, where the best features of public, private, and permissioned are combined. An example of such a network is Corda.[1]

Let us consider some analogies to illustrate various combinations of governance and permissions in controlling a network and access to services. Please note that all the following are examples of centralized systems where we need to trust, for example, the mobile operator that it does not, for example, intercept our communications. Such a trust cannot be assumed, so there are strict regulations and legislation for the mobile operators and service providers to assure neutrality, privacy, and quality of service.

Mobile networks:
- Network control: private – by the mobile operator; permissioned – only the mobile network operator manages and controls the network.
- Service access: public – anyone can become a mobile network user. The access is non-discriminatory, even though it is not free.
- Service access permission: permissioned – if a user has a subscription, that is, a post-paid plan.
- Service access permission: permissionless – if a user has no subscription, pre-paid.

Open public WLAN:
- Network control: private – by the WLAN provider; permissioned – the provider usually restricts access to the WLAN management system.
- Service access: public.
- Service access permission: permissionless – no user credentials are needed.

Airport public WLAN:
- Network control: private – by the WLAN provider, permissioned.
- Service access: public – anyone can register and then use the service.
- Service access permission: permissioned – users need some prior registration, for example, through a web page.

Company private WLAN:
- Network control: private – by the company running the WLAN, permissioned.
- Service access: private – only registered company employees can use the service.
- Service access permission: permissioned – users need a WLAN account provided by the WLAN administrators.

Various permission levels can be applied in a network (Table 2.2). Some of the activities might require registration and an appropriate permission level (e.g., adding new full nodes). Some might be prohibited entirely (e.g., the mining). The others might require no special permissions by the user (e.g., creating accounts and issuing transactions).

---

1 https://www.corda.net

Tab. 2.2: Permissioning approaches in public, consortium, and private DL networks.

	Public	Consortium	Private
Network control and operation			
Adding network nodes	Permissionless	Permissioned or limited to consortium members	Permissioned
Mining and consensus	Permissionless	Limited to consortium members	Not possible
DL service access			
Accounts and transactions	Permissionless	Permissioned or permissionless	Permissioned or permissionless
Node API	Permissionless	Permissioned or permissionless	Permissioned or permissionless

2.3.1.3 User and data privacy in DL networks

Privacy is another challenging concept when DL networks and services are scrutinized. The permissionless nature of many known public DL networks might lead to the idea that anonymity and privacy are intrinsic features of (all) DL systems. We have to distinguish between [21]:

– User privacy; and
– Data privacy

In permissionless public networks, user privacy is assured. Anyone can create a new account in such a network and send and receive transactions from it. The network does not require any mapping between the user's personal identity and the DL network account/address. Unless the user himself discloses the ownership of a particular account, this remains private and anonymous. This is frequently done when users register with an online crypto exchange to buy and sell cryptocurrencies for established fiat money, such as EUR or USD, and then conduct DL transactions to their other DL accounts.

However, the data about all the transactions related to these accounts is entirely transparent. A copy of the ledger and thus the entire content of the blocks and transactions are publically available, as this is the fundament for distribution and decentralization of the DL system. In such a network, data is not private at all. Anyone can follow all the incoming and outgoing transactions for any account or calculate the account balance.

The same limitations to data privacy apply in private and consortium-based networks, just that the access to data is not fully public but reduced to those in control of the network. Data privacy in DL networks can be assured, but appropriate techniques have to be adapted. One of them is zero-knowledge proof. See Section 3.1.1 for

ZK-SNARK and other privacy-related approaches in DLT-based IoT solutions. Even with the transaction-related privacy that is enabled, transaction auditing is possible to comply with anti-money laundering or tax regulations, where disclosure is under the user's control.

2.3.2 Network performance

It is challenging to be address DL performance systematically and in an ordinary way because it intertwines many divergent technologies, network implementation, performance criteria, or use-related expectations.

Transaction throughput (number of transactions per second, tps) and transaction confirmation latency (delay) are the two most straightforward performance metrics. However, it is difficult to compare even these two metrics among different DLTs or networks. Transaction throughput and latency of current DL systems cannot be compared to the figures of the centralized or traditional distributed database services [22]. Often, much of the bad user experience can be related to misconceived perspectives or insufficient understanding of the underlying technology, or inappropriately chosen use cases for the DLT. Besides, it is impossible and unfair to judge the performance of a DLT based on (only) one network implementation. For example, the Ethereum technology performance cannot be estimated only on the quantitative experience (measurements), for example, the Ethereum mainnet. The same technology (same software) can be implemented in a private or consortium network. Different network sizes or settings assure dramatically different performance in terms of transaction throughput or latency. This is true for all DLT architectures, where different deployments are allowed.

It is often hard to obtain relevant and comparable performance results. Theoretical limits can be calculated. But realistic performance stress tests in live public networks are difficult to be executed, for example, due to transaction costs. Analyses of smaller private networks with the same DLT cannot fully mimic large distributed ones. Furthermore, some DLT and network providers are approaching performance aspects of their systems systematically and backed by research (Hyperledger Fabric [23]) and tools (Caliper) (Fig. 2.4). Others provide transparent and detailed statistics about the network (see Section 2.6.4). Some merely present impressive figures that cannot be replicated and lack transparent methodology.

Apart from transaction throughput and latency, several other metrics become important with real-world network deployments and DApps. These include DL network energy consumption, resource requirements put on nodes (e.g., storage for the chain data) and off-chain clients (e.g., transaction generation-related encryption in constrained IoT devices), or transaction costs.

2.3.2.1 Transaction throughput and latency

Transaction throughput is the number of committed transactions in a given time interval. However, not every unit of the work process counts as a transaction, in this case. Only transactions that result in a state change should be considered. Examples of such transactions are transferring funds from one account to another in Bitcoin (BTC) or invoking a smart contract call via the transaction in Ethereum. The smart contract read requests are not executed with state-changing transactions, so they should be excluded from this metric. This is also true for the pass-through transactions, where the same transaction is passed among various smart contracts. It should be therefore counted as one. Invalid transactions rejected by the validating node and, thus, do not qualify for inclusion in the ledger should be excluded, too. This might seem obvious, but there are network performance reports where it is impossible to determine what actions were counted and what were not.

The overall transaction latency depends on times needed for:
1. transaction generation, that is composing the data structure, calculating hashes
2. submission through an access node
3. propagation over the P2P network and validation of the transaction in the miner
4. block creation and the consensus in the network
5. extra time to reach a sufficient level of finality.

The first two factors reflect the off-chain factors, such as the resources of the end device that is generating a transaction. The remaining factors reflect the network performance.

The theoretical limit for transaction throughput can be calculated from the average block time and the average number of transactions in a block. Block time distributions depend on the consensus algorithm. In PoW, the block time is a consequence of the current block difficulty and the overall hashing power of the network. The difficulty is automatically adapted to the changes in hashing power, but the jitter in block times is always present in PoW. The Proof of Authority (PoA), on the other hand, can provide very consistent block times because the target block times a setting in the PoA network genesis. Blocks in a blockchain carry a limited number of transactions. In the BTC network, the maximum block size is 1 MB. With an average size of 500 B, the maximum number of transactions is about 2,000 per block. A new block is produced about once every 10 min. This results in an average BTC network throughput of 3 tps. In Ethereum, the sum of gas (see Section 2.3.2.3 for gas and transaction costs) of all transactions in a block has to be less than the maximum gas (per block). In the Ethereum mainnet, with the maximum block size of 10,000,000 and minimum gas per transaction of 21,000 (or average gas 72,000), there can be up to 476 (138 for average size) transactions in a block. A new block is generated, on average, in 13 s. The maximum transaction throughput of the Ethereum mainnet is about 37 tps (10 tps for average size).

The block time cannot be simply reduced for better performance (both higher throughput and lower latency) without jeopardizing network convergence. If the consensus algorithms require broadcasting block creation information through the network (e.g., in PoW), the propagation delay depends on network size. Extensive network size is needed for high distribution and decentralization. If the block time were reduced close to or under the network propagation time, this would lead to constant forking at the end of the chain and, possibly, to network divergence.

The network transaction latency is the time needed for the state change caused by the transaction to be reflected across the network – the time difference between submitting a newly created transaction and confirming inclusion in the ledger. Two events have to be distinguished in the transaction lifecycle. A transaction is first confirmed by a miner when it is included in a newly mined block. However, it is not guaranteed that the block will become a part of the chain until the information is propagated and accepted by the network. This is when the transaction is finalized. In a network with only one mining node, confirmation and finalization occur at the same time. The network transaction latency is calculated per transaction, but we mainly provide statistics over several transactions, such as the average, maximum, minimum, and standard deviations.

Finality assures that the transactions cannot be arbitrarily changed or reversed after being validated and included in blocks. In DL networks with probabilistic finality (BTC, Ethereum), we cannot reach a 100% finality. Instead, the time for a transaction to be considered as finalized is the amount of time one has to wait for an appropriate guarantee. For sufficient finality, we, therefore, wait for confirmation of additional blocks (usually 2–10) to be appended after the one with our transaction. In DLT architectures with absolute (or deterministic) finality, once the block is confirmed, all transactions in a block are immediately considered finalized. For networks in which not every block is finalized, a useful metric is a delay between the latest finalized block and the current latest block. This number shows how much validators are lagging behind, agreeing on the correct chain [24].

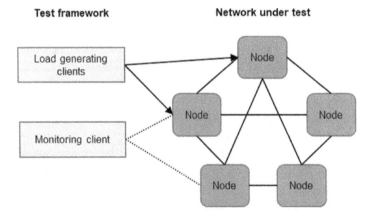

Fig. 2.4: System for DL network performance evaluation.

Public DL networks rely on different network topologies, which influence the network performance. Often, this is at the cost of decentralization and security. BTC and Ethereum are both highly distributed networks, with thousands of mining nodes, where network propagation is relevant for the consensus and performance. To reduce the effects of network propagation times and thus increase the odds for successful mining, mining pools apply more efficient protocols for information propagation within the pool. In Hedera Hashgraph, only ten mainnet nodes execute a form of virtual voting to reach a consensus on both the validity and the timestamp of every transaction. The voting selects a single miner to choose the next block. The community of nodes running Hashgraph then comes to an agreement, as a collective, on which transactions to add to the ledger. In the EOS[2] blockchain network, the number of block producers is low, too. There are 21, which take turns in producing blocks in a round-robin fashion. Anyone can start his/her EOS node and, if voted for by the community, can become a block producer. To select these 21 block producers, users vote on a list of candidates (Delegated Proof of Stake (DPoS)).

2.3.2.2 Resource consumption

Running and using a DL network can mandate significant resource requirements, including computation, storage, and energy.

The PoW consensus mechanisms are known to be highly energy inefficient (see Section 1.2 for details). The hashing power provided by the mining nodes requires high computational capabilities (CPU, GPU, or dedicated hardware). The annualized energy consumption[3] needed to run the BTC network is comparable to a mid-sized developed country. Therefore, it is not surprising that energy efficiency is one of the critical objectives of alternate consensus mechanisms. This is especially true for private and consensus governed networks, where the mining process is not monetarily incentivized or compensated.

The chain data size in BTC and Ethereum is hundreds of GB and is constantly growing. In a P2P file-sharing system, a network participant can keep and share only a small portion of the content, for example, only a specific version of the installation file for a popular Linux distribution. The participant does not have to share the entire content (all the installation files available) to be a meaningful member of the distributed network. In DL networks, on the other hand, one has to keep and share the entire distributed ledger because this is the only way to assure decentralization and trust in the system. This requires substantial dedicated storage for a full node. Large storage requirements deter many enthusiastic net citizens from setting up a reliable full public DL network node and contributing to the system's decentralization. Large

---

2 https://eos.io/
3 https://www.cbeci.org/

chain size also increases the bootstrap time needed for a new node to synchronize with the chain.

Communication requirements for a non-mining and mining node are rather diametric. The chain synchronization requires reliable but modest bitrate network connectivity for a network node. The average data for the regular synchronization of new blocks in the Ethereum is about 18 kB/s and about 10 kB/s in download [25]. Intermittent connectivity is essential for the off-chain applications, which may cease to run or run properly, with the chain unsynchronized due to temporary connectivity problems.

For overall network performance, the rapid dissemination of block-related information between the mining nodes is essential. Block propagation time can become the critical performance bottleneck in truly distributed networks with many participating mining nodes. Distributed communication protocols applied for this propagation are not the most efficient and are sensitive to any low-level communication-related propagation delay. Therefore, a capable, low-delay communication is recommended to interconnect the mining nodes. Many of the mining pools apply dedicated communication approaches to speed up the dissemination of mining information within the pool and, in this way, gain some advantage for the miners of their pool.

Other computer resource demands, for instance, memory and CPU power needed to run non-mining full network nodes or network access clients, are usually not very restrictive if we set these nodes on regular computers. However, with IoT devices, which are often constrained in computation and communication resources, this quickly becomes a problem. We review the details of the blockchain and IoT in Section 3.

At this point, we would like to explain the gas, which is used to evaluate the resource consumption of smart contracts and transactions in Ethereum. Gas reflects both the size of a transaction (in bytes) and the complexity of the calculations during the smart contract execution. However, gas reflects only the complexity of state updates and smart contract execution. It does not reflect all the resources needed, for example, for validating a transaction and is thus unsuitable as an exact indicator of the overall network performance [26].

2.3.2.3 Transaction costs

DL networks adopt wildly divergent approaches to compensate the capital expenditures and operational costs (Table 2.3):

– Compensation as a reward for successful mining. This approach is the key compensation principle in large distributed public networks, e.g., BTC and Ethereum. Due to the immense costs of energy, financial rewards for miners are necessary. For a successfully created block, which is appended to the ledger, the miners newly create the agreed amount of cryptocurrency and register it to their accounts. Mining rewards are gradually decreased. This is a built-in function of the DL protocols.

- Compensation through transaction fees. In DL networks with public cryptocurrencies, the transaction fee is charged to the transaction sender. This is additional charge to the bounties for successful mining. For a long time, the mining rewards were higher than the transaction fees for a block. However, in Ethereum, the transaction fees for a block have already matched the mining reward. Various principles exist to determine the actual fee.
- Participation in transaction validation. In some DLTs (e.g., IOTA), the transaction submitter must validate one or more transactions from other submitters. In this way, the load and the costs related to transactions are distributed directly to the senders.
- No compensation through the DL network. This is convenient for private or consortium networks with a low distribution of the network nodes where the overall costs are not very high. The network providers seek other means for income, for example, charging other services based on the DL network or contributions from the consortium partners. In this approach, the transaction senders pay no fees.

There is no absolute value of acceptable transaction costs, as this varies from use case to use case. In decentralized finance (DeFi), application costs of several EUR or USD might be acceptable. On the other hand, in micropayments and microtransactions, even a fraction of a cent may be disputable and limiting for a successful use case. Apart from the absolute value, the volatility of the fees can be a problem.

Tab. 2.3: Transaction costs in various public DL networks.

	Type of cost compensation	Key characteristics
Bitcoin	Transaction fees based on transaction size in bytes	Fee depends on the fluctuations of cryptocurrency value
Ethereum	Transaction fees based on gas	Fee depends on fluctuations of cryptocurrency value
Hedera	Fees for network services API calls	Predefined rates set in fiat
Corda	Annual participation + transactions fees	Predefined rates set in fiat
IOTA	Participation in the validation process	The sender has to do the PoW for two previously unconfirmed transactions.

Transaction fees in BTC need to reflect the transaction size in bytes. As the BTC block size is limited, miners may prefer smaller to large transactions. They are, therefore, motivated to prioritize the smaller ones. On the other hand, a transaction sender can prioritize a transaction with a higher fee. Many crypto wallets have already come up with built-in fee calculators.

The transaction fee in Ethereum is determined through gas and gas prices. Gas reflects resource consumption and, thus, the costs of processing a transaction. A transaction sender selects the gas price (value in Ether). The gas is multiplied by the gas price to calculate the fee of a particular transaction. It is more likely that miners will consider a transaction with a higher fee while building the next block.

As all the Hedera Hashgraph network services are available only through APIs, users cannot directly create and submit transactions. They would rather pay for the API calls instead of paying fees for transactions. The API pricing is transparent,[4] and the fees are set in fiat. They vary according to the type of API call. The crypto transfer API call was priced in 2021 at 0.0001 USD, allowing micro-transactions (<0.01 USD) to be economically and technologically practical. A smart contract call or a creation of a file in the Hedera DL costs 0.05 USD.

A separate entity called Corda Network Foundation was set up to govern the development and networks in Corda. In Corda, the networks are semi-private and permissioned. A node must obtain a certificate from the network operator to join a network. A network operator would charge reasonable costs for providing network and administration services, which is paid by the Foundation. In Corda, the participants pay an annual participation fee and transaction fees. Transaction fees are charged for notarization provided by Corda Network notary and are structured in two different models: Pay-As-You-Go and Up-front package. The total fees depend on the number of transactions, but Corda provides a very transparent and predictable transaction pricing.

IOTA replaces transaction fees paid in terms of MIOTA (or another digital asset, or fiat) with transaction fees paid in terms of hash power.[5] The sender of a transaction has to establish the PoW for two previously unconfirmed transactions. This way, mining is distributed among transaction senders and not among dedicated mining nodes. In IOTA, transactions are then reinforced when other transactions reference them. Currently, transactions only become truly valid (finalized) when the network Coordinator, a special node operated by the IOTA Foundation, confirms them.

2.3.3 Scalability

We need to investigate the scalability in the context of two additional blockchain properties, all three together known as the blockchain scalability trilemma. This trilemma points out three essential properties of DL systems: decentralization, security, and scalability. Decentralization (see Section 2.1 for more details) refers to the diversification in ownership and control in the DL system. The degree of decentralization is

---

4 https://www.hedera.com/fees
5 https://aakilfernandes.github.io/whats-wrong-with-iota#false-claims-of-free-transactions-and-no-mining

not a binary attribute, and practical network implementations provide some level of decentralization between fully decentralized and (fully) centralized systems. Security includes network operation aspects that make the network robust and resilient to attacks (e.g., 51%, DoS). Scalability is about expanding the network in terms of additional nodes, and more importantly, increasing its performance.

Decentralization, security, and scalability aspects cannot easily co-exist, so balancing them is needed (Fig. 2.5). For example, in an extensive public network, increased distribution and decentralization provide a higher level of trust but increase security risks from anonymous and possibly malicious network participants. Similarly, more centralized governance in a consortium-based network can be favorable to scale the network performance, but it reduces the (decentralized) trust.

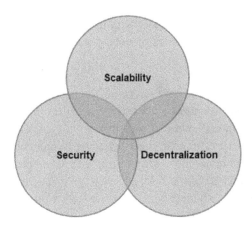

Fig. 2.5: The scalability trilemma in the blockchain.

With the extensive increase of users, performance and scalability issues of major PoW-based public blockchains has arisen. This has led to the research of novel DLTs and affected the development of the existing ones. Several approaches can be taken to facilitate scalability in blockchain systems. We discuss three scaling principles, which are being implemented in various forms and for different existing blockchain technologies:

- On-chain scaling solutions include modifications in the ledger (block size and structure, block times), consensus mechanism (see Section 1), or sharding of the network.
- Off-chain scaling solutions attempt to facilitate transaction off-loading, that is, a trusted transaction exchange out of the main ledger, for example, with the state channels and oracles.
- Cross-chain scaling solutions where multiple DL networks are interconnected via gateways/relays to exchange transactions among various systems. Cross-

chain solutions are a very novel research area. They not only contribute to the scalability of DL networks but are also crucial for DL interoperability.

2.3.3.1 Sharding

Sharding is an on-chain method, where the DL network topology is divided into several smaller networks, called shards. Each shard contains a part of the network nodes. Different shards process transactions in the network. This reduces the number of transactions that have to be processed by each node and has two positive consequences:

- State sharding – nodes keep only data of their shard. This reduces the nodes' system requirements and reduces the bootstrap time.
- Transaction sharding – transactions are distributed among different shards; they can be processed and verified in parallel. This increases the transaction throughput of the entire network. A reduced number of nodes in a shard accelerates the block propagation, too.

But such a change of network topology has several difficulties. For the performance increase obtained with sharding, we sacrifice decentralization and thus the trust in the system. Distribution is also reduced, so common DL network security risks (51% attack) become emphasized. Another problem is that of transactions originating in one and destined to another shard. These cross-shard transactions are more difficult to be processed. They require more communication and dedicated mechanisms to propagate between the shards. Therefore, the efficiency of sharing is strongly dependent on the statistical properties of the transactions and, thus, on a particular use case.

A modified sharding approach consists of the main chain (network) and multiple shard chains. Each shard periodically commits its state to the main chain. In this way, the trust in the shard data can be verified. The cross-shard transactions are processed via the main chain. The efficiency of this approach suffers enormously, if the number of cross-shard transactions increases and the main network becomes a bottleneck.

Research on sharding investigates how to allocate nodes into shards efficiently and how to protect decentralization and security. Most of the sharding development and implementation focuses on public DL networks, often, those with PoW consensus. In private or consortium networks, performance is increased, instead, by trimming the main network operation.

2.3.3.2 Off-chain state channels

State channels are a complementary off-chain method that temporarily off-loads the transactions between two DL accounts from the DL network into a dedicated channel. State channels are also known as payment channels, if the transactions predominantly exchange value between accounts and not tokens or smart contract calls. They reduce the load of the main chain and thus improve the performance of the overall system. A channel is established, managed, and cleared through a smart contract in the main DL network, which serves as an arbiter. It can be established directly between the two accounts. A channel can have several hops through the state channel network in a dedicated off-chain network of state channel nodes, which build a layer on top of the DL network. As the transactions in the channel are not built into blocks, there is no latency due to block creation, and no transaction fees apply.

Two prominent examples of state channels are the Lightning Network[6] for BTC and Raiden Network[7] for Ethereum. The Lightning network is limited to BTC transactions. Apart from regular transactions, the Raiden network supports ERC20 tokens, too.

2.3.3.3 Cross-chain swaps

Cross-chain techniques, also known as the atomic swap, or cross-chain atomic swap, have a twofold role in DL network topology and operation:

- Scalability – they separate transaction exchange from a single common DL network into a set of interconnected networks. As the transactions are distributed into several networks, they can be processed in parallel. This increases the transaction throughput of the entire system.
- Interoperability – unlike in sharding, cross-chain swapping can integrate networks based on different DLTs, so that the DL applications are no longer confined to their chains.

Its interoperability is even more disruptive than the contribution to scalability, as it is opening a range of new DL use cases. In this way, we will be able to assure protocol and semantic interoperability between BTC, Ethereum, and other DLT-based networks. Similarly, we could integrate, for example, a private and a public DL network into a hybrid topology. Through the cross-chain swap, the smart contract service flows in the private and in the public network remain synchronized, as if the entire platform were implemented in one network. Still, with two (or more) network types, we can now support different performance, security, and scalability requirements of the overall business logic.

Cross-chain swaps are assured through elements called relays, bridges, and hubs, usually along with a dedicated DL for relaying. COSMOS[8] is an ecosystem of connected blockchains. It utilizes a DL network based on the Tendermint Core with the Cosmos consensus mechanism. The Inter-Blockchain Communication (IBC) protocol is used to connect to other DL networks and applications. Polkadot,[9] too, is a

---

6 https://lightning.network/
7 https://raiden.network/
8 https://cosmos.network/
9 https://polkadot.network/

relaying blockchain. With a set of validators, it assures the security of the relaying chain, which links together various independent parachains. Collators are network elements that link to already running DL networks, including Ethereum. They package the parachain blocks and pass them to validators for verification.

2.4 Smart contracts

Smart contracts are the second cornerstone of the DApp triplet (see Section 2.2 for details). The term smart contract was coined in 1996, long before the appearance of the first blockchain networks, by Nick Szabo [27]. He regards smart contracts as contractual closes, which are implemented in hardware and software in such a way as to make a breach of a contract prohibitively expensive. He pointed out vending machines and traditional payment or banking transaction systems as forerunners of modern DApps and smart contracts. Interestingly, from the principles in law, economic theory, and contractual conditions often found in practice, he outlined four basic objectives of the contract design [27]:
- Observability – the ability to prove one's or to observe other's performance of the contract
- Verifiability – proving to an arbitrator that a contract has been performed or breached
- Privity – minimizing the vulnerability to third parties and excluding them from the knowledge and control over the content and performance of the contract (privacy and confidentiality)
- Enforceability – minimizing the effort for enforcement, including self-enforcing protocols

Szabo so well anticipated many of the findings, which, several years later, implemented his ideas in the BTC protocol and network that he is considered as one of the candidates for the real BTC inventor. The real inventor remains unknown and is still known only by the pseudonym Satoshi Nakamoto. At least to some extent, the four mentioned objectives are met in most of the current DLTs and networks that reach beyond the simple value transactions and enable DApp development (Ethereum, Hedera Hashgraph, and Hyperledger).

Smart contracts are neither smart nor binding in the sense of legal obligations. However, in business collaborations, they are typically used to enforce some type of agreement, so that all participants can be certain of the outcome, without an intermediary's involvement [28]. Such an agreement, coded in the smart contract on-chain logic, has no central point of failure, can perform operations, hold value, and unlock it only if specific conditions are met [29, 30].

2.4.1 Virtual machine

The execution environment for the smart contract code can be compared to a virtual machine, which is provided by the DL network. In fact, in Ethereum, this environment is called the Ethereum Virtual Machine (EVM).

Different virtual machines exist for the currently available DLTs. EVM is among the most popular ones. Some of the non-Ethereum DLTs adopted the EVM, too, despite having completely different ledger and consensus technologies from Ethereum. For example, Hedera provides an adaptation of EVM implementation for the Hedera Smart Contract Service. Sawtooth,[10] one of many Hyperledger projects, with its built-in Hyperledger Burrow,[11] can run Solidity smart contracts in the EVM for Hyperledger. This not just facilitates the reuse of smart contracts developed for Ethereum; using the same smart contract programming language and relying on a familiar smart contract execution environment can also be very favorable for the developer. They can rely on their preceding software and security engineering experience and reuse their existing codebase, making the development faster and more secure.

Other DL virtual machines take different approaches and use different smart contract programming languages. The smart contract code in Corda, for example, is written using Kotlin, a programming language from JetBrains that targets the Java Virtual Machine (JVM) and JavaScript. The virtual machine for contract execution and validation is an augmented and radically more restrictive version of the JVM, which enforces security requirements and deterministic execution. Smart contracts in EOS run WebAssembly, meaning that a wide variety of languages is supported. The chaincode in Hyperledger can be written in any programming language and is executed in containers. Currently, Golang, JavaScript (in NodeJS), and Java chaincode are supported. With the provided support for EVM, Hyperledger can also run Solidity smart contracts.

The distribution of a DL system does not scale the performance of a VM. Each node in the DL network (not just miners) executes the smart contract code. This ensures the consensus and, thus, trust in the results of the smart contract execution. All DL nodes repeat the same operation coded in a smart contract, and thus all run the same copy of the virtual machine. Smart contract processing capabilities of the whole network, therefore, remain limited to the capabilities of a particular node.

---

10 https://www.hyperledger.org/use/sawtooth
11 https://www.hyperledger.org/use/hyperledger-burrow

2.4.2 Lifecycle

A smart contract is a software product. Its lifecycle is being designed and developed, compiled, and deployed to the DL network. Finally, it is used as a part of a DApp. This is similar to any other software product. However, smart contract execution in the DL network imposes several specifics and limitations in smart contract software engineering related to development, performance, and security. We will discuss these in the following sections. The smart contract lifecycle is outlined in Fig. 2.6. It is indicated in the figure that the management and several phases can be found in the lifecycle, too. However, these are not necessarily present, if the smart contract is very simple or software engineering is taken lightly. Omitting the verification and thoroughly planned and implemented management of smart contracts can have devastating security consequences. The figure refers to the lifecycle that is typical for the Ethereum-based DApps. Smart contracts in other DL platforms might have slightly different lifecycles. For example, in Hyperledger Fabric, no compilation of smart contract source code into BC native executable bytecode is needed, as the smart contracts are installed and run in containers.

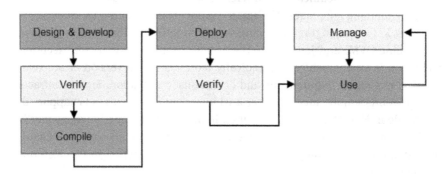

Fig. 2.6: Smart contract lifecycle in Ethereum.

Design, development, and source code verification produce the source code of a smart contract. In Ethereum, source code is usually coded in the Solidity language (see Section 2.4.3 for details on smart contract tools and languages). During the design and programming of the source code, different formal and runtime methods can be taken to verify the correctness of the smart contract code and minimize possible security flaws in the specification and code implementation.

The source code is then compiled to a version that can be deployed and executed in the DL system. In Ethereum, this is an Ethereum-specific binary format, called the EVM bytecode.

In Ethereum, the use of a deployed smart contract is defined by an Application Binary Interface (ABI) specification [31]. An ABI is an interface between external program modules and the smart contract bytecode. The bytecode and the ABI file are then sent off to the blockchain with a contract creation transaction. This special transaction is sent to an empty receiver BC address, with the EVM bytecode as data. The transaction sender is a valid Ethereum account. This account becomes the owner of the smart contract. Once the smart contract deployment transaction is added to the chain by validating nodes in the BC, the smart contract obtains a unique smart contract address. Now, transactions can be destined to the address of the newly deployed smart contract. A smart contract has its balance, some code, and some persistent storage to execute its operations. Another level of verification can be added after the deployment. We can now check for possible compilation flaws at the bytecode level or ensure that the deployed bytecode logic matches the source code.

In the Ethereum BC, the ABI stipulates the de facto mechanism for encoding/decoding data into/out of a smart contract, that is, how we call functions in a contract or pass and get data back. Slightly different approaches are taken in other distributed ledger architectures, for example, Hyperledger [32]. Other smart contracts in the network and the external (off-chain) applications call smart contract methods to read the smart contract parameters or send BC transactions to the smart contract to change its state. A smart contract can emit events filtered by the DL network nodes and can be passed to the external applications by a node. Different smart contracts in the same network reside within the same virtual machine. Their communication is straightforward and limited only by the access rights encoded in a smart contract. Off-chain applications need to have access to a valid DL account and an API to communicate with the DL node. For the Ethereum off-chain applications, several frontend JavaScript APIs are provided, including frontend programming libraries. An example is the Web3.js – Ethereum JavaScript API,[12] a collection of libraries that allows interacting with a local or remote Ethereum node using HTTP, IPC, or WebSocket.

It is very common for the traditional Web applications to access various resources on the Internet, using various protocols, for example, HTTP, HTTPS, WebSockets, WebRTC, RPC, and others. On the other hand, the smart contract execution environment limits the scope of the smart contract execution to the DL network. A smart contract can only call other smart contracts in the network but cannot access resources out of the DL.

The smart contract methods can be accessed in two ways by the DL network participants. Suppose an off-chain application or another smart contract requires, for example, a simple read of a smart contract parameter. In that case, this is done with a local invocation (occurring only in the local DL node) of the smart contract method. On the other hand, when a DL network participant needs to modify some state in the smart contract, the call must be initialized through a transaction sent to

---

12 https://web3js.readthedocs.io/en/v1.2.11/

the smart contract address. This transaction can include a cryptocurrency for the smart contract and additional input parameters for the method call. Transactions have to be validated and included in the chain in the same way as non-smart contract transactions. Upon inclusion, the smart contract is executed, and the state (of the contract and the entire ledger) is updated accordingly. The smart contract's bytecode, of course, remains unchanged. Any code changes of the deployed bytecode are impossible due to the DL's immutable nature.

Fig. 2.7: Class diagram of a simple single-contract smart contract solution.

Figure 2.7 shows a class diagram of a simple single-contract solution, which provides two methods, the promoteToAdmin, and poeCreate. The first expects a parameter hopefulAdmin with a value corresponding to the Ethereum address of the new administrator. The poeCreate method receives a hash value and contextual data about this hash. These methods are executed with the given parameters. If encoded conditions are met, the poeCreate method emits an event called poeCreated, which is intercepted by all the nodes in the blockchain network, and notifications are given to the off-chain applications that are subscribed to these events. The hash in the poeCreated event is indexed, so subscribers can request to be notified only of poeCreated events with a specific hash. The smart contract also includes a number variable called eventCount, which is publicly readable.

2.4.3 Smart contract programming

Most of the DL smart contract execution environments, including Ethereum, Hashgraph, and BTC, follow state machine replication on the *order-execute* principle. The consensus mechanism of these DLTs assures a clear order of the smart contract-invoking transactions before their execution. The ordered transactions are then executed sequentially on all peers, reflecting in the common change of the ledger/smart contract state. For this to happen, the execution of smart contracts (processing of all transactions address to a smart contract by the smart contract's code) needs to be deterministic.

The requirement for deterministic execution places a strong limitation on what a smart contract can do. For example, using date or time functions, generating random values, or retrieving data from off-chain resources (e.g., external API calls) prevents deterministic execution. It is, therefore, very common that these DLTs use special smart contract programming languages to enforce the determinism even at the level of programming language. Suppose the deterministic scripting language used by the VM is Turing-complete. In that case, this essentially means that the types of smart contracts that the developers can design are limited only by their programming skills and creativity.

However, not all DL smart contract execution environments follow the order-execute principle. Hyperledger applies a different transaction lifecycle and, therefore, different smart contract execution and validation principle. It is called execute-order-validate [33]. The name indicates that a smart contract call, invoked by a transaction destined to a smart contract address, is first executed. The transactions to smart contracts can therefore be executed in any order, possibly, in parallel. A transaction need not be executed by every node in the network. After a transaction is executed, endorsement policies define which nodes need to agree on the result of a transaction, and then it is added to the ledger. This is the phase where transaction ordering occurs. The transaction validation, which happens last, is separated from the execution. During validation, each node has an ordered list of already executed transactions and can check if any of them is invalid, for example, due to double-spending.

The execute-order-validate approach has several relevant benefits. These are increased performance (not every node executes every smart contract), smart contract code privacy (only the endorsement nodes need to know the smart contract code), and the possibility of using general-purpose programming languages for smart contract development.

2.4.3.1 Languages

Various programming languages are applied to develop smart contracts, depending on the VM in the selected network. Some VMs support diverse programming languages for smart contracts and others stick to one.

Ethereum uses deterministic programming languages Solidity (prevalent) and Vyper for smart contracts. Solidity, the most popular language[13] on Ethereum, was inspired by C++, Python, and JavaScript, and Vyper is based on Python. One can build smart contracts in JavaScript, C++, or Python. Still, because of the order-execute constraints and contexts related to the EVM, it is easier to have a language specifically for the task.

---

13 https://ethereum.org/en/developers/

EOS[14] blockchain network supports WebAssembly (WASM) for smart contract programming, despite being an order-execute DL, too. WASM is not deterministic, so it is up to the programmer not to use any non-deterministic input like the time of a day or random number generator.

Hyperledger Fabric is the first blockchain system that runs smart contracts written in general-purpose programming languages, such as Go, Java, Node.js. The smart contract code is executed in containers.

2.4.3.2 Tools and libraries

At the beginning of the DApp era, only a basic set of tools with limited functionality was available for the developers. Most of the tools were related to Ethereum and Solidity – the cornerstones of the pioneering DLT for DApps. The development tools were mostly desktop or online code editors, with added Solidity code highlighting and syntax checking. Some were linked to the Solidity compiler, while others left the compilation to other tools. Debugging was manual, and there were no or only very basic security validations available.

With the maturing of DApp ecosystems, new tools and frameworks appeared more integrated and provided broader functional scope. These tools support the development, validation and testing, and deployment of smart contracts. We are now approaching the development environments with similar maturity as those for, for example, long-established Web application development.

For Ethereum, dedicated frameworks (Truffle) and integrated development environments (IDE) (e.g., Remix) exist. Popular multi-purpose development environments (e.g., VS Code) support coding, compilation, and security validation of Solidity code, too. These tools and frameworks can be integrated with code validators (MythX) or emulators (Ganache) for preliminary testing in emulated blockchain networks. The same tools can be used for smart contract development for Hedera Hashgraph because it implements Ethereum's EVM and uses the Solidity for smart contract programming. The EOS ecosystem, too, sustains a broad set of development and testing tools[15] for their smart contacts. Integrated with various tools required for EOS in a unified graphical application, EOS Studio, for example, provides a powerful and easy-to-use environment for DApp development.

Besides, Solidity has some inbuilt libraries, which enhance the security or implement some of the common functionality frequently used by many smart contract developers in a systematic and proven way. This speeds up the development process and enhances security. However, the application of external libraries might contradict the desired simplicity of the smart contract code and introduce possible new risks with additional code in the library. Some of the libraries are:

---

14 https://eos.io/
15 https://developers.eos.io/welcome/latest/community-developer-tools/index

- Modular network: includes many modular libraries like ArrayUtils, Token, Crowd-Sale, Vesting, StringUtils, LinkedList, Wallet, and so on
- OpenZeppelin:[16] provides role-based access control (library called Roles) and secure mathematical library (SafeMath) as well as other security-related libraries for smart contract programming for Ethereum (MerkleProof, ECDSA, Address, SafeERC20, Arrays)
- DApp-bin: was created by Ethereum and included libraries like DoublyLinked-List, StringUtils, IterableMapping, and so on

Various levels of code testing are essential for efficient and secure (see Section 2.4.4 for more details) smart contracts. Several projects aim to formal verification of smart contracts, and a comprehensive list is being maintained [34]. Some of these tools operate at the source code level (i.e., the Solidity), whereas others operate at the compiled bytecode level. MythX[17] is a cloud-based smart contract security service. It performs security analysis remotely, accepting jobs and returning results via an API. It currently detects most weaknesses found in the SWC Registry. It, thus, covers assertions and property checking, byte-code safety, authorization controls, control flow, the correctness of ERC standard implementations, and various coding best practices for Solidity [35]. The analysis types include symbolic analysis, fuzzing (bytecode), Solidity code analysis, taint analysis, and static analysis. The MythX API has been integrated into many development frameworks, including Brownie, Truffle, Remix, and VC Studio. OYENTE [36] is another tool to analyze the Ethereum smart contracts code, based on symbolic execution. OYENTE takes two inputs, the Ethereum smart contract bytecode and Ethereum global state. It checks a contract against several known software weaknesses. Although the majority of the testing tools aim toward Ethereum and Solidity, other DL technology ecosystems address this issue, too. Chaincode scanner [37] is a static security checker for Hyperledger Fabric smart contracts. It takes a chaincode written in Go as input and checks it for nine vulnerability patterns.

Other tools can facilitate the development and monitoring of the deployed smart contracts. Chain and block explorers are presented in Section 2.6.4. A valuable tool is the Hyperledger Caliper,[18] which is a part of the Hyperledger endeavors. The Hyperledger Caliper is a benchmarking tool, which allows users to measure the performance of a blockchain implementation with a set of predefined use cases. The Hyperledger Caliper produces reports containing several performance indicators, including resource utilization, transaction latency, and transactions per second (tps). Besides several Hyperledger DLTs, the Caliper benchmarks Ethereum-based networks, too.

---

16 https://openzeppelin.com/
17 https://mythx.io
18 https://www.hyperledger.org/use/caliper

The Hyperledger DL ecosystem (see Section 2.7.1.2) develops and promotes several business blockchain libraries. For example, Hyperledger Ursa[19] is a shared cryptographic library, which enables implementations to avoid duplicating other cryptographic work and increases security in the process.

2.4.4 Smart contract security

Smart contract security and the security of the related DApps are parts of a broader cybersecurity landscape (Fig. 2.8). They, therefore, share many known risks and vulnerabilities commonly found in other ICT systems and applications, too. Such common attack vectors are, for instance, attacks on the application clients, attacks on user-wallet credentials through phishing, dictionary attacks, or by exploiting bugs in hardware wallets. The same holds for the exploits of digital signatures, hash functions, or address vulnerabilities. Distributed denial of service (DDoS) attacks can target the DLT and DApp infrastructure, for example, the off-chain application parts or the auxiliary services, such as crypto exchanges and mining pools.

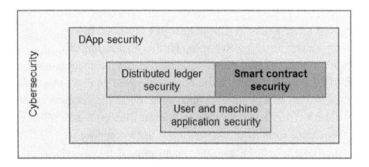

Fig. 2.8: Smart contract security and cybersecurity.

However, in addition to the common cyber risks and vulnerabilities that affect DApps due to the decentralized and distributed nature of DLT, unknown, specific vulnerabilities and risks appear or become severely augmented. Possible attacks and new attack vectors comprise the governance and operation of the DL network, mining and consensus, tampering of transactions, and attacks on smart contracts. Various vectors are frequently combined into one attack area to gain control over the network, a part of the network, or individual nodes and then exploit this control to manipulate transactions. Some of the attack vectors might be extremely difficult and costly to execute. In truly decentralized DL networks, they might be practically almost infeasible. However,

---

19 https://www.hyperledger.org/use/ursa

in more centralized (private) networks, the risks remain real. Many of the attack vectors are protocol- and implementation-specific and are not present in every variant of DLT, so the actual implementation of a DL network may mitigate or prevent some of the risks with, for instance, high decentralization, authorized nodes instead of anonymous ones, consensus mechanisms other than traditional PoW, and so on.

While some of the defense mechanisms and mitigation techniques are already available in other ICT domains and readily available in modern software development lifecycles, others need to be newly developed or adapted to the DLT. This is not surprising. Most of the DLT platforms, tools, and smart contract programming languages are still in their infancy, often, fast-evolving and constantly changing the features. Hence, design flaws might exist in the DL platforms or smart contract languages. Along with DLT ecosystems, security approaches mature, too.

The immutable nature of a previously deployed smart contract code exposes vulnerabilities that could be easily mitigated in traditional software systems but can present severe risks in decentralized applications. As with any source code, even a thoroughly tested and validated smart contract might have bugs. Design flaws may exist in blockchain platforms or smart contract languages. Common Software Security Weaknesses (CWE) [38] may be amplified on blockchain platforms and in the related smart contract security [39]. Such weaknesses include improper behavioral workflow, access control or initialization, incorrect calculation and insufficiently random values, the inclusion of untrusted external functionalities (e.g., external libraries, smart contracts deployed by others), and improper exception handling and cryptographic understanding.

Key smart contract vulnerabilities stem from logical flows, bugs in the smart contract code, and under-optimized code patterns. Logical flows in the implementation of the contract, where, for example, a smart contract does not refund the initial deposit, lack of cryptography for user inputs to ensure fairness, or incentive misalignments [40], can be deliberate or caused by a misunderstanding of distributed ledger properties. In public DL networks, where cryptocurrencies and miner awards are part of the DApp execution, there is a risk of under-optimized smart contract code patterns that lead to unnecessary gas consumption [41]. Their research states that the two main reasons for this are useless code-related and loop-related patterns.

In Ethereum, smart contract vulnerabilities arise from the Solidity language, the Ethereum or EVM blockchain platform, and a misunderstanding of common practices. In Hyperledger Fabric chaincode, vulnerabilities arise from almost identical points: the Go language, the blockchain platform, and a misunderstanding of common practices.

2.4.4.1 Smart contract weakness classification

The Smart Contract Weakness Classification and Test Cases Registry (SWC Registry) [39] is a comprehensive list of key security flaws in the Solidity smart contract code. It provides a checklist for smart contract programmers and many of the smart contract vulnerability detection tools. Possible vulnerabilities are labeled as SWC *x*, where *x* is the vulnerability index, for example, SWC 107.

Some common Solidity smart contract vulnerabilities include transaction-ordering dependence, timestamp dependence, mishandled exceptions, and reentrancy. Transaction-ordering dependence (SWC114) can be a problem if users have no control over the order of transaction execution. The order is up to miners. If there is more than one transaction that invoked the same contract, the order of those transactions can affect the new state of the blockchain. Timestamp dependence (SWC116) is related to smart contracts and includes conditions that are triggered by the block timestamp. Block timestamps are set by miners based on their local system time and can be unreliable or manipulated by an adversary. Mishandled exceptions (SWC104) target the contract that calls another contract. If any exception occurs in the called contract, it terminates and returns false, but it may not notify the caller contract. Reentrancy vulnerability (SWC107) is present when a contract calls another contract, and the current contract execution waits until the called contract finishes. This provides an opportunity for the adversary to exploit the intermediary state of the caller contract and call its methods, several times. Authorization through tx.origin (SWC115) could make a contract vulnerable if an authorized account calls into a malicious contract. A call could be made to the vulnerable contract that passes the authorization check since tx.origin returns the original sender of the transaction, the authorized account.

2.4.4.2 Steps to securing smart contracts

We can take two types of security measures to secure smart contracts – passive and active smart contract security. Both subsets are not exclusive or replacing one another but have to be seen as two independent cornerstones of smart contract security. Passive security measures entail smart contract architectures, software engineering techniques specific to the smart contract environment, or code reviews and verification (see Section 2.4.3.2 for tools and libraries for smart contract programming). Active measures occur during smart contract execution and refer to smart contract and method access control, active monitoring of the incoming smart contract transactions, and authorizing their actions.

2.4.4.2.1 Updating and upgrading

As discussed at the beginning of Section 2.4.4, the immutable nature of a previously deployed smart contract prevents the simple replacement of the existing code with an updated or upgraded version. Of course, we can always deploy the new version to the blockchain network. However, the original smart contract has to be rendered unusable, usually by disabling any transactions addressed to it. Consensys highlights several Ethereum Smart Contract Best Practices. To assure an effective upgrade path for bug fixes and improvements, they advise mechanisms to pause, freeze, or delay smart contract actions and mechanisms to migrate and transfer data and funds to the updated version of the smart contract. Two software engineering techniques[20] can be applied in case of an emergency, if relevant flaws are found after the deployment. Circuit Breakers pause or stop smart contract execution if certain conditions are met. They can be useful when new errors are discovered after the deployment. Most contract functionality may be therefore suspended, and the only action now active, is a withdrawal. We can either give certain trusted parties the ability to trigger the circuit breaker or have programmatic rules that automatically trigger certain breakers when certain conditions are met. Speed bumps delay or slow down contract actions, so that if malicious activities occur, there is time to recover.

2.4.4.2.2 Modularization

In modern software engineering, source code is usually split into modules. These modules are easier to handle and navigate than all of the lines of code contained in a single file. Modularization makes the management of software easier, including updates and upgrades. The code is reusable, and functions are separated. The bigger the code base gets, the more sense it makes to have a multi-contract architecture and the greater the security benefits to the service become.

However, modularization is not a common practice in smart contract development. Smart contract usage patterns in a large set of Ethereum-based DApps indicate that about 75% of Ethereum-based DApps apply very simple single contract architecture, meaning that the on-chain application logic consists of only one smart contract. The remaining DApps are multi-contract, on average comprising three smart contracts. Therefore, the efficient reuse is very limited, and the smart contract source code is mostly simply duplicated among different implementations. Single contract solutions may meet the functional demands of the users but often result in unmanageable decentralized applications when the requirements for updates arise.

The Diamond approach to upgradeable modular contracts has been proposed as the Ethereum Improvement Proposal (EIP) 2535.[21] This draft document proposes a proxy contract that supports using multiple logic contracts. These delegate contracts are called facets, and each facet supplies one or more functions. A dedicated function enables adding, replacing, or removing functions. Events are emitted upon changes in diamond functions, and a user can verify what version of the function is called. With this design approach, one can develop and incrementally improve the smart contract logic of a DApp over time. However, the design of smart contracts ownership, authentication, and authorization is not a part of this draft.

Modular contracts can be upgraded in a controlled manner. Several approaches can be taken, or auxiliary services can be used to do this, for example, a registry contract, delegate calls, or Ethereum Name Service (see Section 2.6.3 for name services).

---

20 https://consensys.github.io/smart-contract-best-practices/software_engineering/
21 https://eips.ethereum.org/EIPS/eip-2535

2.4.4.2.3 Example of modularized smart contract architecture for DApps

Modular smart contract architecture requires a set of smart contracts to work together as the on-chain part of a decentralized application. Therefore, the security and access policy for the contract methods has to be carefully designed and planned. It makes sense to have a dedicated smart contract that handles access control and interaction permissions for all smart contracts in a decentralized application. This means that all security is centralized and offers a better overview than having access and security policies defined in every smart contract in the multi-contract architecture.

We can now separate the service-specific and service-agnostic functions into separate modules. Service-agnostic modules provide key platform functionalities required in any multi-contract solution. A directory module can serve as the single access point, that is, the only interface for the external users. It automates the dissemination of the addresses in other smart contract modules. If one of the contracts in the deployed system is upgraded and replaced, the directory reflects this change and transparently directs the remaining contracts to the updated address. An administration module provides common access control for all the smart contracts and methods in the solution.

Service-specific modules depend on the DApp objective and provide unique functions for service operation, for example, in the management of distributed energy resources (see Section 4.3.3.1) or car park reservation (see Section 4.2.2), or decentralized collaboration between robots (see Section 3.6).

Auxiliary modules provide additional functions relevant to service provisioning. However, their functions, such as loyalty tokens, asset tokenization, escrow service, or value collection, are common and relevant for other application verticals, too. Therefore, auxiliary modules can be provided system-wide and reused in various decentralized applications.

Modular architecture with a separate access administration module allows us the definition of various tenants. Although they all interact with multiple modules using the interface smart contract, they are only allowed to call some methods, while the other methods are restricted. Typically, the tenants in a decentralized application would be, for example, application owners, administrators, service providers, and service users.

2.4.4.2.4 Secure multi-contract interactions

The Diamond standard (see Section 2.4.4.2.1) proposes an upgradeable multi smart contract environment, but it does not include any security mechanics that would provide secure and reliable inter-smart contract interactions. We can extend this basic modularization with secure smart contract tunnels (SCT) [42]. Smart contract tunneling introduces twofold access control: per module (only registered modules can interact) and per user. The administrator tenant sets up the tunnels in the directory and administration modules. With the directory module, we can always assure that the method call was passed through an authorized module and that it originated from an authorized smart contract account. We use both the tx.origin value to verify that a transaction originated from an authorized source and msg.sender value to verify that the transaction was forwarded from an authorized source.

Figure 2.9 depicts a tunnel set up between the interface contract and subsequent target smart contract. Only smart contracts, which are properly registered in the directory and authorized in the administration module, can access the target smart contract in our multi-contract solution. In addition, the transaction origin address in both interface and target smart contract can be checked to limit the access to the particular method, according to the tenant roles of a specific user. The unregistered smart contract cannot send transactions to the target.

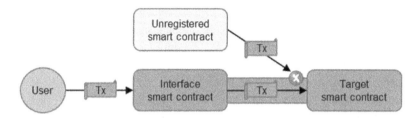

Fig. 2.9: Smart contract tunneling for smart contract module access control.

2.5 Off-chain applications

In the decentralized application triplet (see Section 2.2), DL network nodes assure all the blockchain-specific protocols for network operation and functions for interaction with other nodes in the network and on-chain smart contract execution. The Web, mobile, server-side, or embedded off-chain applications need to interface with these nodes to utilize the blockchain-specific features and services provided by the DL network.

Therefore, some of the network nodes expose blockchain APIs – usually JSON-RPC or REST interfaces – for software applications to interact with the DL network. We can enable the API for blockchain service access as an option on our node in a public permissionless network. Alternatively, we can rely on third-party APIs for public DL networks, provided as a service (see Section 2.7.2.2) for more efficient productization of decentralized applications. In permissioned networks adding nodes might be more restricted and limited to authorized users. The restrictions are motivated by network security and ledger data privacy, with some DL networks not allowing any nodes to be added at all. In these cases, the APIs are the only mechanism for external entities to participate or interact with the network. For example, to access Hedera services (see Section 2.7.1.3 and Section 1.4.), mirror nodes are used. One cannot run a mirror node in Hedera, but Hedera and community mirror nodes are available, with APIs for Hedera services.

The API endpoints in public networks commonly impose no access control to the off-chain applications. Lack of access control might seem surprising if we compare it to the API access in many other Web-based applications. Nevertheless, since the ledger is shared and available to all involved parties, there is no need to protect access to it. Blockchain account-related operations, which can lead to severe security vulnerabilities, are performed in the off-chain application parts. If we establish some access control for the node API, it is mainly to protect the node's computing resources.

2.5.1 Off-chain application examples

Off-chain applications utilize the established Web, mobile, server-side, or embedded applications technologies to provide user and machine interfaces for the DApps.

Apart from the node APIs, blockchain ecosystems usually provide off-chain client libraries for different programming languages. These convenience libraries abstract much of the complexity of interacting with blockchain node APIs.

Despite a remarkable resemblance between traditional and blockchain-enabled Web user interfaces, the blockchain backend introduces several usability problems. They are mostly related to the BC transaction latency. Therefore, users cannot always count on refresh rates and response times expected in traditional Web applications. Consequently, it is a good user interface design principle to notify the user when we await a longer response than expected due to the DL network interaction. For example, we can temporarily redirect a user to chain explorer (see Section 2.6.4) for live tracking of his transactions during that period.

Another blockchain backend effect on off-chain Web, server, or embedded applications arises from blockchain node API queries. We cannot form the node API requests as efficiently as in, for example, relational databases. Therefore, the number of requests to a remote API might become substantial, if the client application design does not consider this possibility. This can result in increased node-resource consumption and unnecessary communication load between the client-side application and the API. The latter might be especially challenging in communication-constrained embedded IoT blockchain applications.

2.5.1.1 Client-side web applications

Client-side Web applications run in browsers. Apart from the execution of client-side application logic, the browser must include a key wallet. A wallet enables the management of blockchain keys and identifications. It can be an integral part of a browser (e.g., Brave[22]) or a browser extension. Metamask[23] is a popular wallet extension for Ethereum-based networks. Figure 2.10 shows the Metamask menu, where we can toggle between available Ethereum networks, including the Mainnet and various public test networks. With Metamask, we can also attach our browser to an Ethereum node running on the local computer or specify a URL to an arbitrary JSON-RPC node API. In this way, we can access, for example, private or consortium networks with the Ethereum DLT.

Fig. 2.10: Metamask wallet extension in a Web browser.

A common convention in the Ethereum Web application ecosystem is for key management software to expose their API via a JavaScript object in the Web page. The EIP 1193[24] formalizes an Ethereum Provider API to promote wallet interoperability. The API is designed to be minimal, event-driven, and agnostic of connectivity and RPC protocols. Its functionality can be extended by defining new RPC methods and message event types.

---

22 https://brave.com/
23 https://metamask.io/
24 https://eips.ethereum.org/EIPS/eip-1193

In the client-side application, developers apply client libraries for BC node API interactions, for example, Web3.js[25] for Ethereum Web applications, and create their application-specific programming logic. Web3.js is a collection of libraries that allows us to interact with a local or remote Ethereum node using HTTP, IPC, or WebSocket.

In this way, we can use all the available Web-interface technologies (HTML5, CSS, and JavaScript) or frontend frameworks to create rich, interactive, and modern Web user interfaces that utilize blockchain features. These user interfaces interact with live blockchain networks.

2.5.1.2 Web-server or embedded application parts

We must arrange the blockchain key management differently, if the software running in a server or an IoT device needs to interact with a blockchain node API. No human will toggle among the available blockchain networks or provide the wallet-access authorization credentials. Still, we might need a key store in such an application. Still, we usually set the DL network and the account information only during the initial configuration of the server-side application.

On the other hand, the interactions with the BC node API are very similar to the ones in client-side Web applications. If we develop, for example, a Node.js backend application or IoT device software, we include the same Web3.js library (see Section 2.5.1.1) for Ethereum Web applications. Off-chain application development for Ethereum is not limited to JavaScript. Web3.py[26] is a Python library for interacting with Ethereum. Originally, it was derived from Web3.js but has since evolved toward the needs of Python developers.

2.5.1.3 Mobile applications

A very similar approach is taken in mobile platforms, too. There are mobile Web browsers and mobile browser wallet plug-ins available. Metamask, for example, runs on Android and iOS, too. This facilitates access to the same Web-based blockchain application as for the desktop browsers.

Web3j.io[27] is a lightweight, reactive, type-safe library for Java, Android, Kotlin, and Scala, if we develop mobile applications that do not rely on browser functionality.

---

25 https://web3js.readthedocs.io
26 https://web3py.readthedocs.io
27 http://web3j.io/

2.5.2 Distributed ledger node APIs

Blockchain node APIs range from pure REST APIs (e.g., Hyperledger Fabric) to JSON-RPC (e.g., Ethereum) with the usual connectivity methods including HTTP, WebSocket, and IPC. Not all of them are necessarily present in all DLTs or even in different node implementations for the same DL network. Approaches also differ in the set of features provided through the API. But they commonly offer information about the node client, blockchain network, blocks, and transactions, provide account management, and enable the creation and submission of new transactions.

2.5.2.1 Ethereum JSON-RPC API

Ethereum JSON-RPC API[28] is the API for Ethereum node implementations. Not all the implementations assure the same feature set. In Tab. 2.4, we provide a brief comparison of connectivity methods in some of the dominant nodes. The combination of JSON-RPC and HTTP is common for all of them. IPC and WebSockets are supported only in some cases. Suppose we design a decentralized application, which specifically relies on, for example, a WebSocket connection, we must account for the possibility that not all network nodes will be configured for DL network access or that adaptations will be needed to migrate from one blockchain network to another.

Tab. 2.4: JSON-RPC support in various Ethereum node implementations.

	Cpp-ETH	Go-ETH	Py-ETH	Parity	HL Besu
JSON-RPC 1.0	+				
JSON-RPC 2.0	+	+	+	+	+
HTTP	+	+	+	+	+
IPC	+	+		+	
WebSocket		+		+	+

Ethereum JSON-RPC API has a single endpoint, for example, http://localhost:8545. The API method, along with the corresponding parameters, is embedded in a JSON structure submitted to this endpoint. The Ethereum JSON-RPC API enables selecting features and gives detailed information about network status, including number and details about the connected peers. Account management returns a list of addresses owned by the client. These accounts must be enabled when we start the node. The API provides detailed information about ledger synchronization, including block and transaction details. We can create, sign and send new transactions to

---

28 https://eth.wiki/json-rpc/API

the network. We could set and manage event filters used to track interactions with smart contracts in the network through the API, or manage the mining if it was enabled in the node.

2.5.2.2 Hyperledger Fabric REST API

Hyperledger Fabric nodes facilitate a RESTful API service. The CoreAPI[29] is composed of several endpoints, which reflect the APIs functionality. We select the appropriate HTTP method to choose between creating, reading, and deleting the selected resources.

The root endpoints are /block, /chain, /chaincode, /network, /registrar, and/ transactions. We use /block API to retrieve the contents of various blocks from the blockchain and the /chain API for the current state of the network. The /chaincode endpoint is used to deploy, invoke, and query a target chaincode, that is, the Hyperledger Fabric smart contracts. It implements the JSON RPC 2.0 specification and must have the required fields supplied within the payload. The /network gives information about the network of peer nodes comprising the blockchain network. As the HLF networks are permissioned, the /registrar manages end-user registrations. We can use the /transactions/{UUID} endpoint to retrieve an individual transaction matching the UUID from the blockchain.

2.5.2.3 Hyperledger Sawtooth REST API

Hyperledger Sawtooth API[30] also relies on the proven RESTful service approach. It systematically utilizes HTTP status codes to provide detailed feedback about the execution of a particular API call.

2.6 Distributed and support services

Several services extend the functions of the core DLT and its on-chain logic in smart contracts. These services are not mandatory for DL network and DApp operation but make it easier, provide more control, and facilitate architectural refinements, welcome by the users.

Decentralized blockchain storage facilitates large quantities of data that would be unsuitable or impractical for the storage limitations of a regular blockchain. Name services add an additional layer of addressing or naming in DLT. They abstract the immutable DL network addresses and enable user-friendly naming. These names can be remapped to new DL network addresses if, for example, a smart contract address has changed. For smart contracts to interact with off-chain external data sources,

---

29 https://openblockchain.readthedocs.io/en/latest/API/CoreAPI/#rest-api
30 https://sawtooth.hyperledger.org/docs/core/releases/1.1/rest_api/endpoint_specs.html

special trusted gateways called oracles are needed. Moreover, chain explorers help us examine and analyze the content of the distributed ledger in a live blockchain network. They aggregate and display data from network nodes in a human-readable and user-friendly way.

2.6.1 DL-based storage

The core application of blockchain technologies, a distributed ledger, is just distributed, safe, and trustworthy data storage. As we discussed, this has many different uses in a variety of applications. However, many other applications require bulk data storage or file storage. This data cannot be written directly to the blockchain because it would greatly inflate the size of the ledger itself, hurting the performance of the chain in the long term.

There are several distributed blockchain-based storage solutions available, each with its characteristics [43]. Some core concepts are shared between them. These concepts are storage methods, replication, and incentives for hosts. Data is stored in a very similar way. Each file is split up into small pieces called shards. Each shard is encrypted before being stored on a machine that is part of the storage network (not the actual blockchain network). Only the locations and hashes of these shards are then stored on the blockchain network. Having relatively small and uniform pieces of data also helps improve storage and transmission efficiency. The machines that these shards are stored on eventually have many shards of data of identical size.

Another shared concept is data replication. The data needs to be protected in the case of network failures. This means all shards need to be replicated across several machines. The exact number of replicas varies, but 3 is, generally, the minimum used. Since the shards do not have an easily identifiable connection between them, there must be a mechanism to ensure that the data is sufficiently replicated across the network.

In traditional cloud storage infrastructure, files are stored with a company that can charge for the services provided. Public distributed systems are composed of many different small hosts and have no single entity to carry out actions like issuing invoices. Therefore, each distributed data storage system needs to have a way of rewarding the hosts of files. This varies from technology to technology, but some examples reward the owners with tokens or cryptocurrency that have value or give them more power to vote on the system.

Swarm[31] is Ethereum's answer to blockchain-based storage and is designed to work in the Web3 ecosystem. Shards (called chunks in Swarm) of files are stored across multiple Swarm nodes, with a manifest stored in the main Ethereum blockchain

---

31 https://swarm-guide.readthedocs.io/

network. Swarm nodes are just Ethereum nodes with an extra enabled mode of operation. They keep shards of files and make sure the shards are securely stored and accessible.

Files in the system can never actually be changed or deleted by the user. Instead, the user uploads a new file and changes the ENS reference to point to the new file. Swarm uses Ethereum's cryptocurrency to charge users for storage and reward hosts.

IPFS[32] or Interplanetary File System is a more general distributed file system. It can be used together with various blockchain networks or can be even standalone. To access IPFS, a user must install an IPFS client. Once installed, users and applications can interact with IPFS with HTTP requests sent to this client. Protocol Labs, the organization behind IPFS, is also working on Filecoin, designed to be the incentivization layer, providing nodes with an economic incentive to host data reliably.

Storj[33] is designed to look and perform like object storage from traditional cloud providers, but with a decentralized backend. Applications generally interact with it via its S3-compatible API. It uses its blockchain-based system with STORJ tokens as an incentivization method.

2.6.2 Oracles

The deterministic smart contract code is executed in a blockchain virtual machine. The execution is isolated from external, real-world environments, and the contract state is maintained and determined by actors inside the blockchain systems [44].

Despite the decentralized and trustless architectures of the blockchain systems, smart contracts on their own cannot access data from the external world. Oracles are needed to integrate smart contracts with the real world, if the non-deterministic smart contract code requires external information to make decisions. The real world, in this case, implies external software, hardware, or human actors and inputs they are providing to be used in the on-chain application parts. Software resources can be, for example, Web APIs from a weather data provider or real-time or historic price-pairs for financial applications. Hardware resources could be an IoT sensor device, contributing sensory inputs, or physical device identifiers, for example, RFID tag values, for a supply chain or a manufacturing management DApp. Human actors can provide inputs in the form of an answer to questions, their voting decisions, and the like.

Oracles collect and provide data feeds and input to smart contracts. On the blockchain, oracles are represented by smart contracts that serve data requests from other

---

32 https://docs.ipfs.io/concepts/
33 https://www.storj.io/

smart contracts. Oracles assure data attestation for these diverse off-chain sources and bring external data into the blockchain system in a trusted, verifiable way.

Figure 2.11 depicts the high-level oracle architecture. Decentralized application (see Section 2.2) comprises a blockchain network with a smart contract execution environment, blockchain-aware user interfaces, and DApp smart contracts. Oracle is an intermediary between the smart contract environment and external resources. It can request data from external sources, receive external data feeds, or keep historical records data values. It assures the validity of these data and serves it to the DApp smart contracts when needed.

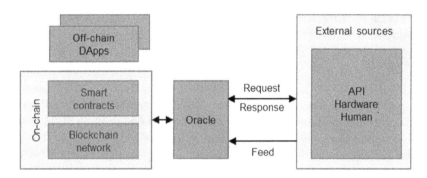

Fig. 2.11: High-level oracle architecture.

There are two key trust models available to verify and validate the external data. In the centralized oracle trust model, only one node is used by the oracle solution to get data into a smart contract. Therefore, this node needs to be trusted. This model is appropriate for data in the external world that cannot be independently validated by multiple distributed parties, for instance, because the data has restricted access or is transient sensor data. Examples of centralized validations in oracles are, authenticity proofs (TLSNotary) for software oracles and trusted execution environments (TEE) for hardware oracles. The alternative is the decentralized oracle trust model. Here, the methods such as decentralized reputation, voting, or consensus-based decisions assure a common agreement about the external data source. Both models are used in practical oracle implementations to meet the distinguishing features of various external sources.

In any case, oracles are off-chain architecture components that could be points of failure in whole blockchain-based systems. Even if the DL network and the on-chain smart contract application are highly reliable and trustworthy, there is always a risk of oracles providing corrupt, malicious, or inaccurate data. Oracle security is, therefore, an emerging research area. Several oracle solutions have been proposed and implemented.

Provable[34] is a blockchain agnostic oracle service for smart contracts and blockchain applications. It has been integrated with platforms like Ethereum, Rootstock, R3 Corda, Hyperledger Fabric, and EOS. It provides feeds to smart contracts from sources that include arbitrary URLs (any webpage or HTTP API endpoint), random results coming from external TEE compliant hardware, computation results from the Wolfram Alpha computational engine, or file content on the IPFS network. External data is delivered in a certified process, where authenticity proofs give transparency to the execution, and external audits verify that Provable code does what it should do.

To implement the Provable service, DApp developers and the users of such applications do not have to trust Provable. It acts as an untrusted intermediary. Optionally, a request to Provable can specify authenticity proof. Data providers do not have to modify their services to be compatible with blockchain protocols. Through Provable, smart contracts can access data from the existing Web sites or APIs.

Town Crier[35] system leverages trusted hardware (Intel SGX) to provide a strong guarantee that data comes from an existing, trustworthy source. Town Crier (TC) obtains data from target websites specified in queries from application contracts and uses SGX to achieve its authenticity. If we trust SGX, data delivered by TC from a website to an application contract is guaranteed to be free from tampering. If we can trust the execution environment, we can trust that data delivered by TC from a website to an application smart contract is free from tampering.

Augur[36] is a P2P protocol for blockchain-based prediction markets, in which users receive payouts when they predict a winning outcome. The technology is predominantly used for betting applications. However, Augur acts as a decentralized oracle,[37] too. After the betting event has occurred, the outcome of the event is determined by Augur's oracle. Results are determined by Augur's oracle, which consists of profit-motivated reporters who report the actual, real-world outcome of the event. Reporters use a staking token (REP or reputation) to clarify disputes on outcomes of the prediction. Anyone who owns REP may participate in the reporting and disputing of outcomes. Users lock REP tokens in escrow, thereby staking them to assert the outcome of a particular created market. A specific incentive structure is incorporated in Augur's platform that rewards reporting on correct outcomes and penalizes reporting on incorrect outcomes. This builds trust in the oracle data.

Chainlink[38] enables smart contracts on any blockchain to leverage extensive off-chain resources, such as tamperproof price data, verifiable randomness, external APIs, and much more. Various decentralized Chainlink oracle networks guarantee the

---

34 https://provable.xyz/

35 https://town-crier.org/

36 https://augur.net/

37 https://github.com/AugurProject/whitepaper/releases/latest/download/augur-whitepaper-v2.pdf

38 https://chain.link

authenticity of external input data and the resulting output events. The Chainlink network, for example, provides tamper-resistant and high-quality price feeds, furthering the growth of DeFi.

2.6.3 Name services

Given the immutable nature of blockchain technologies, accounts, data, and code cannot be changed or deleted. This means that whenever developers want to update a smart contract on a blockchain or a site hosted on Ethereum Swarm, they have to create a new one, which, of course, has a new unique identifier, that is, the Ethereum address. On the user side, the latest versions of a website or smart contract need to be always available at the same name, and this is preferred to be human-readable. Traditional systems use DNS to solve this issue, binding human-readable names to IP addresses and simplifying back-end migrations, load balancing, and geographical optimizations.

Ethereum Name Service (ENS) fulfills many of the equivalent needs present in the Ethereum ecosystem. It binds human-readable names to hashes like Ethereum addresses and Swarm file identifiers. This is a key part of making DApps more accessible for regular users. ENS is a system of smart contracts, each responsible for its own subdomain. Several top-level smart contracts in the system (as for .eth and .test) that further smart contracts are registered as resolvers. A resolver could be registered with the .eth top-level smart contract with the name ethereum.eth, so any queries for it would first go to the .eth smart contract and then get directed to the ethereum.eth smart contract. This can be arbitrarily chained for ENS names like wallet.ethereum.eth. All interactions with the top-level domains in ENS are done strictly through the smart contracts and the methods they provide. This provides a high degree of transparency and trust. The cost of a .eth domain in 2021 was 5 USD in ETH per year for 5-character names and longer, 160 USD for 4-character names, and 640 USD for 3-character names.

The process of registering a name on ENS takes five days and requires multiple time-sensitive transactions. When we want to register a name, a public auction is opened instead of the name simply being purchased. The name itself is hashed, so only people who know the name can participate in the auction. The auction lasts for 72 h and is followed by a reveal phase in which bidders must reveal their bids. If they do not, their funds are lost. The winner must pay an amount equivalent to the second-highest bid on top of their bid to get the name. Losers get their bids back.

The relation between the registry and resolvers is depicted in Fig. 2.12. ENS can be queried[39] through the Etherscan chain explorer.

---

39 https://etherscan.io/enslookup

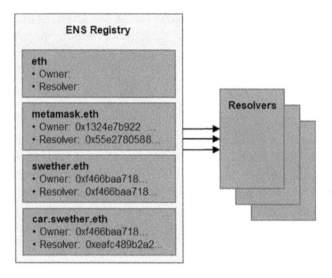

Fig. 2.12: Ethereum Name System registry and resolvers.

Apart from ENS, which names smart contracts, several DNS-like registrars are based on decentralized applications. These systems are completely independent of the traditional DNS and ICANN. Registration is managed directly by users, and name resolution is generally made through a browser extension. Unstoppable domains[40] manages the .crypto and .zil domains and are based on Ethereum technology. Namecoin[41] is a fork of BTC that focuses on storing and managing key-value pairs distributed securely. The key is a human-readable name and a value that is an address. It provides a DNS-like service for the .bit domain.

2.6.4 Chain explorers

Chain explorers are tools used to examine and analyze the DL in a blockchain network. They aggregate and display data from network nodes in a human-readable and user-friendly way.

Given the application architecture considerations associated with chain explorers, these are generally Web applications with separate pages for viewing assets like accounts, transactions, and smart contracts. They also show important network statistics as well as an up-to-date feed of blocks and transactions.

Several similar tools are often available for the same network, mainly provided by a trusted first party, like the network operators, or by an unconnected third

---

40 https://unstoppabledomains.com/
41 https://www.namecoin.org/

party, like an open-source project group. This is a great example of the openness of public blockchain-based DL networks.

Either way, they are useful as a second opinion into the state of the chain. The DApp will often provide links to these tools to give users a way to independently verify that the transactions did occur the way the application showed, providing an extra layer of trust. Since these DApps use a blockchain-based backend, chain explorers are, often, key in identifying and fixing issues.

Etherscan[42] is the most popular chain explorer for Ethereum. A snapshot of the user interface is given in Fig. 2.13. A similar tool called Hyperledger Explorer[43] also exists for Hyperledger Fabric.

2.7 Productization of DApps

When an enterprise considers adopting decentralized technologies in digitalization or aims to provide new DLT products or services to the market, selecting the underlying DLT platform is a strategic decision. During this adoption, investments in the ICT infrastructure and services might occur; acquisition and training of skillful personnel are needed, as are considerable investments in the DApp development. Therefore, the enterprises seek long-term and sustainable solutions and partnerships. For the appropriate strategical decision, one needs to evaluate and compare particular DLT products or technological platforms and the entire ecosystem. The apt choice can lead to faster adoption of technical solutions, decreased initial development and long-term progression expenditures, and reduced support costs. This then results in technological and business advantages and the generation of new sources of revenue.

Technological platform characteristics are, of course, vital. The characteristics of DL networks, for example, performance, governance, and scalability, depend on technical differences of the DL and details of network implementation (see Section 2.3). Smart contract environments (see Section 2.4) decisively define DApp design and functionalities. However, many additional aspects, apart from the platform, represent a DLT ecosystem.

A set of libraries and tools is expected for the development, facilitating the development and testing, monitoring networks, and validating the solutions. Developers need documentation and efficient support, both formal and informal. Some DLT ecosystems provide systematic training programs and certification.

A demonstrated ability to keep with a clear roadmap is a good guarantee that the DApp and the selected underlying DLT platform, tools, and libraries will improve,

---

42 https://etherscan.io
43 https://www.hyperledger.org/use/explorer

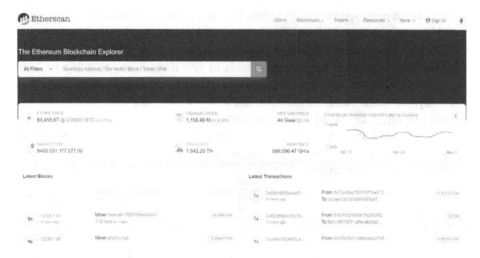

Fig. 2.13: Etherscan – chain explorer for Ethereum.

evolve and receive support in the future. It might also be relevant if a DLT ecosystem clearly anticipates steps, which make its operation green and energy-efficient.

A key decision factor should be the community gathered in the ecosystem. A successful ecosystem attracts and actively supports users and developers. A large, active community shows that the ecosystem encourages an open, collaborative culture. A community with a large global footprint also indicates the level of acceptance of the platform among users and developers. The communities should not be seen only as users or customers of the ecosystem but rather as the external innovators. This attitude proved to be successful, for example, in many open source projects. Therefore, some of the DLT ecosystems have clearly defined mechanisms for collaboration with academia and enterprises.

Finally, the number and scope of prominent use cases are other good indicators of what we can expect from a DLT ecosystem.

2.7.1 DLT and DApp ecosystems

Here, we present a brief overview of some of the available DLT ecosystems. This is, by no means, a comprehensive study. There are many other ecosystems. Besides, many forks of the DLT platforms do not bring completely new and independent technological approaches but modify the existing protocols to achieve some improvements. Others might potentially bring interesting platform solutions in the future but are, at the moment, more at a level of concept proofing rather than business-grade DLT platforms. The selected ones are, in our opinion, relevant DLT ecosystems, which should always be considered as relevant alternatives for DLT selection. Bitcoin is not included in these comparisons. Despite being a DLT pioneer and the basis for a public DL network with the largest market capitalization cryptocurrency, it is not applicable for DApps.

Table 2.5 summarizes some of the key features of the selected DLT ecosystems. It can serve readers as the starting point to match the needs of their anticipated DApp with the matching DLT.

Tab. 2.5: Comparison of selected DLT ecosystems.

	Ethereum	Hyperledger	Hashgraph	Corda	IOTA
Managed by	The Ethereum Foundation	The Linux Foundation	Hedera Governing Council	R3	IOTA Foundation
Type	Open community	Curated open community	Limited public input	Limited public input	Limited public input
Public networks					
Cryptocurrency	ETH	/	HBAE	/	MIOTA
Governance	Public	/	Centralized	Consortium	Centralized
Distribution	Very high	/	Low	(not clear)	Unknown
Private networks					
Possible	Yes	Yes	Yes	Yes	Yes
DApp development					
DApp development	Very good	Very good	Good	Good	Not applicable in v1.0
User and developer communities					
Community	Very large	Large	Relatively small	Financial institutions	Relatively small

2.7.1.1 Ethereum ecosystem

Ethereum is an open-source chain-based DL ecosystem maintained by the Ethereum Foundation. In 2021, it continues to implement a well-thought roadmap towards Ethereum 2.0. It includes important changes in DL protocols, such as moving from PoW to energy-efficient PoS consensus and addressing scalability problems of Ethereum public networks.

The Ethereum blockchain technology is deployed in a large and highly decentralized public network, called the mainnet. Anyone can add nodes, including mining nodes, to this network. In 2021, there were about 7,000–8,000 nodes in the mainnet. A major cryptocurrency is available in the Ethereum public network, making it appropriate for DeFi and IoT or other DApps. Private and consortium networks are possible with the Ethereum technology. They are often used to improve performance and privacy compared to the public network.

Ethereum smart contracts are generally written in Solidity, but Vyper and Flint are also supported. A rich set of libraries, tools, development IDEs, and security validation tools exist for Ethereum decentralized application development. It has the largest developer community. Ethereum is the most popular platform for DApps, including IoT DL applications, with numerous convincing use cases.

2.7.1.2 Hyperledger ecosystem

The Hyperledger ecosystem represents a suite of stable open-source frameworks, tools, and libraries for enterprise-grade blockchain deployments. It involves more than 250 teams and companies and is hosted by the Linux Foundation. The work is organized into projects, which develop different ledger technologies, comprehensive tools, and supporting libraries. The maturity of projects is clearly indicated, as well as their codependence.

Hyperledger's DLs (Burrow, Fabric, Indy, Iroha, Sawtooth) primarily target private and consortium networks. Therefore, there are no public Hyperledger networks, and consequently, no public cryptocurrencies. Only the Hyperledger Besu, a Java-based Ethereum client implementation, can be attached to Ethereum networks. Since Hyperledger networks are meant to support the operations of various organizations, they are private or consortium-based. While multiple organizations might access the same ledger or even multiple ledgers having part of the data exposed to the public, these networks are still considered private. Different approaches to smart contract development are taken in HL, which depend on the selected ledger technology. Hyperledger supports various smart contract programming languages and engines. The most prominent and widely used programming languages are Solidity and Go. Extensive open-source documentation is available for all projects.

Each project has its team of collaborating organizations that vary from world-renowned ICT companies to small teams dedicated to the Hyperledger project development. Prominent Hyperledger use cases include logistics projects, financial projects, humanitarian and philanthropic projects.

2.7.1.3 Hedera Hashgraph ecosystem

Hashgraph is a patented DLT maintained by the Hedera Governing Council. The Hedera Governing Council consists of up to 39 term-limited and highly diversified organizations and enterprises. They reflect up to 11 unique industries, academia, and non-profits, globally. Council members are committed to governing software changes, while bringing stability and continued decentralization to the public network.

The Hedera public network is built on the Hashgraph distributed consensus algorithm. It allows for creating or exchanging value, proving identity, or verifying and authenticating important data. The public cryptocurrency HBAE is available. The cost of a cryptocurrency transaction can remain stable and low, allowing micro-transactions to be economically and technologically practical on Hedera. There are ten mainnet network nodes. Mirror nodes are used to access Hedera services. One cannot run a mirror node on Hedera, but there are Hedera and community mirror nodes available, with APIs for Hedera services. The Hedera network is managed by the Hedera Council and is thus not really decentralized. Hedera smart contracts are not immutable as, for example, in Ethereum. They can be changed if several parties designed by a smart contract developer agree.

From the application developers' point of view, Hedera can be seen as a consortium-based service, exposing decentralized transaction capabilities through APIs rather than a truly decentralized ecosystem.

Prominent Hedera use cases include payments, tokenized assets, and managing credentials.

2.7.1.4 Corda ecosystem

Corda is an open-source DLT developed and maintained by the R3, a technology company that gained prominence in 2015 when a consortium of banks joined the initiative. A separate entity called the Corda Network Foundation was set up, using a not-for-profit legal entity type known as a Stichting to govern development and networks. This type is suited for governance activities and is able to act commercially, with limited liability but no shareholders, capital, or dividends.

Corda networks are private or consortium-based. Therefore, the decentralization depends on a particular case. A Corda network is a permissioned, publicly available P2P network of nodes. Each node represents a legal entity and runs the Corda software. A node must obtain a certificate from the network operator to join a network. This certificate maps a well-known node identity to a real-world legal identity and the corresponding public key. There is no public cryptocurrency in (public) Corda networks.

Smart contracts in Corda are agreements whose execution is both automatable by computer code working with human input and control, and whose rights and obligations, as expressed in legal prose, are legally enforceable. The smart contract code in Corda is written using Kotlin, and the virtual machine for contract execution and validation is an augmented and radically more restrictive version of the JVM. Rich, up-to-date, and well-structured documentation, including code examples, is available to the developers. A rich set of development and monitoring tools is available.

The Corda Enterprise is proven to meet the security, scalability, and support requirements of complex organizations and is now the de facto standard in financial services.

2.7.1.5 IOTA ecosystem

IOTA is an open-sourced DLT developed by the IOTA Foundation. The Foundation has announced an ambitious roadmap towards the IOTA 2.0. It will be a challenge to keep with it. The roadmap envisages a new DL network protocol suite, new wallet, and new library suite and is a major shift compared to version 1.0. Version 2.0 should remove the need for (centralized) Coordinator nodes, add smart contract protocol, and secure messaging and disposable self-identities. IOTA plans to standardize the key DL protocols and has announced collaboration with IEEE and OMG.

In the current version 1.0 of the IOTA network, the transactions are reinforced when other transactions reference them. However, they only become truly valid when the network Coordinator, a special node operated by the IOTA Foundation, confirms them. Due to IOTA's unique ledger style, it has some unique properties. Theoretically, the transaction throughput increases, and the latency decreases as the number of nodes and users increases. The IOTA ledger is distributed, but the network is not decentralized because of the consensus, requiring Coordinator nodes.

There is a public main network and a public test network. IOTA networks use a public cryptocurrency, MIOTA. Transactions are essentially free, but the transaction sender must submit proof of work.

Support for smart contracts is in the alpha stage for v2.0 but is not available in current v1.0, which means that IOTA can only store and transmit data but not process it. This makes it, for the moment, not usable for building DApps. Therefore, IOTA has not attracted a large developer community. Developers would appreciate systematic documentation and clear guidance on how to participate in the IOTA network. Version 2.0 promises relevant improvements but takes immense effort to be finalized and brought to production grade.

2.7.2 Deploying and accessing blockchain networks

DApps require an underlying DL network (see Sections 2.2. and 2.3) for their operation. This can be a new, dedicated private or consortium network that we customize to our needs and construct from scratch. Nevertheless, it could also be an existing prominent public network, where we would like just to attach a couple of additional nodes to participate in blockchain network operations.

A scalable self-provisioned blockchain network is complex to set up and hard to manage. Each node operator needs to manually provision hardware, install software, create and manage certificates for access control, and configure networking components. This can be done as very basic editing of node configuration files, for example, the genesis file. Some manual tasks can be done instead with a CLI wizard, for example, Puppeth, which aids in creating a new Ethereum network. Lately, tools like

Hyperledger Cello[44] – a blockchain provision and operation system – help use and manage blockchains more efficiently. It supports various infrastructures like bare-metal, virtual-machine platforms, and container cloud (e.g., Swarm, Kubernetes).

Once the blockchain network is running, one needs to monitor the infrastructure and adapt to change, continuously. Apart from self-hosted nodes, various Blockchain-as-a-Service (BaaS) providers facilitate efficient blockchain network node deployment and management. Most of the key players in cloud service provisioning, for example, Amazon, Microsoft, Alibaba, and IBM, provide some form of BaaS.

The off-chain DApp parts need to access the DL network node's APIs (Section 2.2 and 2.4.2). These APIs can be exposed in the nodes under our supervision or obtained from a dedicated service provider, for example, Infura. The latter assures reliable infrastructure connecting a user to the Ethereum public network. This is essential for the instant operation of the machine and user interfaces in the DApps. Relying on hosted APIs disengages the application developers completely from the DL network provisioning.

The content of a public ledger can always be obtained through network nodes. However, this might not be the most efficient structure for queries needed in the advanced DL data analyses. Therefore, public datasets of historical data from various DL networks placed in big data platforms make the analysis more efficient.

2.7.2.1 Blockchain-as-a-service

BaaS provides blockchain services in the cloud or edge computing environments, such as node and network deployment, system monitoring, and smart contracts analysis and testing. BaaS implementation outsources a major technical and operational overhead for deploying and accessing the BC network to the cloud service provider. BaaS providers offer adjusted pricing and instance types optimized to fit different blockchain use cases.[45] Based on these services, the developers can focus on the business code to explore how to apply the blockchain technology more appropriately to their business scenarios, without the bother of having to maintain and monitor the blockchain platform [45]. BaaS is improving the productivity of DApp development and initiates a broad adoption of blockchain technologies.[46]

Table 2.6 summarizes the supported DLTs of some of the major BaaS providers. There are two dominant technologies – Hyperledger (Fabric) and Quorum. This is not surprising, since both are predominantly meant for private or consortium-based blockchain networks. Unlike the public networks, these networks are newly deployed, so we have to set up and manage all the network nodes. Hyperledger ecosystem is described in Section 2.7.1.2.

---

44 https://www.hyperledger.org/use/cello
45 https://aws.amazon.com/managed-blockchain/instance-types
46 https://consensys.net/quorum/

Tab. 2.6: Supported DLTs of some BaaS providers.

BaaS providers	Supported DLT
Amazon Managed Blockchain	Ethereum, Hyperledger Fabric
IBM Blockchain Platform	Hyperledger Fabric
Microsoft Azure BaaS	Quorum[47]
Alibaba Cloud BaaS	Ant, Hyperledger Fabric, Quorum
Oracle Blockchain Platform	Hyperledger Fabric

Quorum is an implementation of Ethereum tailored to permissioned enterprise blockchain networks. Therefore, it facilitates DApp development with Ethereum's familiar tools and thus benefits from Ethereum's ecosystem (see Section 2.7.1.1). A Quorum node is derived from the public Ethereum client (Hyperledger Besu – the Ethereum compatible client, see Section 2.7.1.2). It supports a set of additional consensus mechanisms designed with network performance (transaction latency and tps) in mind and enhanced with enterprise features for privacy.

2.7.2.1.1 Amazon Managed Blockchain
Amazon Managed Blockchain[47] is a fully managed service that makes it easy to join public networks or create and manage scalable private networks using the popular open-source frameworks Hyperledger Fabric and Ethereum.

Amazon Managed Blockchain allows us to join public networks (e.g., public Ethereum mainnet) or set up and manage scalable, permissioned private or consortium networks. The service eliminates the overhead required to create the network or join a public network and automatically scales up to meet the demands of thousands of applications running millions of transactions. Once our network is up and running, Managed Blockchain makes it easy to manage and maintain it. It manages authorization certificates and lets us easily invite new authorized members to join the network. This effectively transforms a private blockchain network into a consortium-based one. Managed Blockchain also monitors the network and automatically replaces poorly performing nodes. There are pre-built templates and a BaaS API available for quick node creation.

2.7.2.1.2 IBM blockchain platform
IBM is a founding member of the Linux Foundation Hyperledger Project, collaborating to develop Hyperledger Fabric, so the focus on Hyperledger in IBM Blockchain

---
47 https://aws.amazon.com/managed-blockchain/

Platform[48] is not surprising. IBM Blockchain Platform is a commercial distribution of Hyperledger Fabric and comes with SLAs and full-time support.

Enterprises can connect to nodes running in any environment (on-premises, public, or hybrid clouds) and easily connect a single peer to multiple industry networks. They can deploy only the blockchain components they need (Peer, Ordering Service, Certificate Authority) and manage all network components through a single console, no matter where they are deployed. There is no vendor lock-in, so companies maintain complete control of our identities, ledger, and smart contracts.

IBM Blockchain Platform is working together with the Hedera Consensus Service to increase interoperability, with the latter providing public consensus while a private blockchain network is based on Hyperledger Fabric. The leading use cases based on the IBM Blockchain platform are banking and financial markets, supply chain, health care, insurance, media, advertising, and government.

2.7.2.1.3 Microsoft Azure BaaS

Microsoft Azure BaaS[49] lets us create and configure consortium blockchain infrastructure and rapidly deploy fully managed blockchain networks. It facilitates the Quorum ledger using the Istanbul Byzantine Fault Tolerance (IBFT) consensus mechanism and will eventually support multiple blockchain platforms like Ethereum, Hyperledger Fabric, Corda, and Chaincode.

The service is comprised of three sets of products. Azure Blockchain Workbench is the foundation for building, governing and deploying fully managed blockchain networks and applications at scale. Azure Blockchain Service is a starting point for easy prototyping and simplified development with prebuilt networks and infrastructure. Azure Blockchain Development Kit is a comprehensive GitHub repository of developer blockchain content, including code samples and accelerators. Modular controls provide built-in governance for easy member onboarding, consortia management and codeless permissioning, and simplified policy enforcement. Blockchain data manager enables flexible, reliable, and scalable data streaming and application integration. In this way, users can monitor their smart contracts, react to transactions and events, and stream on-chain data to off-chain data stores to build the desired end-to-end solutions.

2.7.2.1.4 Alibaba Cloud BaaS

Alibaba Cloud BaaS[50] supports Hyperledger Fabric, Ant Blockchain technologies, and Quorum. It provides out-of-the-box services, including enhanced administrative

---

48 https://www.ibm.com/blockchain/platform
49 https://docs.microsoft.com/en-us/azure/blockchain/service/overview
50 https://www.alibabacloud.com/product/baas

---

functions to help us build an enterprise-ready blockchain network environment with ease and without concerns of complex configuration. It includes management of the smart contracts (chaincode) in the organization and the business, including the period of overwriting installation, creating instances, and updating. The platform allows us to create consortia, invite, and approve the participant involved in the business to join the consortium, and manage the business.

Alibaba Cloud BaaS integrates Alibaba Cloud Internet of Things (IoT) and anti-counterfeiting technologies to provide blockchain solutions for product traceability. Other notable use cases stem from supply chain finance, data assets sharing, and digital content ownership.

2.7.2.1.5 Oracle blockchain platform

Oracle Blockchain Platform[51] is a preassembled PaaS, which includes all the dependencies required to support a blockchain network: computing, storage, containers, identity services, event services, and management services. The blockchain network console supports integrated operations.

It is based on the Hyperledger Fabric project from the Linux Foundation, but it extends the open-source version in many ways to meet the needs of enterprise environments. These include, for example, preassembled template-based provisioning, operations monitoring and zero-downtime managed patching and updates, enhanced security and identity management functions, and a set of HL Fabric APIs through REST calls for simpler transaction integration.[52]

Their use cases include large supply chains and trading networks, food safety, retail loyalty rewarding, and identity and voting applications.

2.7.2.2 APIs interfacing public DL networks

BaaS (Section 2.7.2.1) enables node deployments and display APIs for the off-chain applications to utilize the blockchain services. However, BaaS is predominantly meant for private blockchain networks. On the other hand, many uses solely rely on public blockchains, where the network infrastructure is already available. In such a case, reliable remote node services are crucial for user experience in any blockchain-enabled mobile application, blockchain-compatible browsers, and plug-ins for Web applications or blockchain development tools. The developers of these products can completely eliminate the need to install, run, and manage their network nodes for a user to access the public network.

---

51 https://www.oracle.com/blockchain/
52 https://docs.oracle.com/en/cloud/paas/blockchain-cloud/usingoci/

Infura[53] focuses on instant, reliable infrastructure connecting us to Ethereum (mainnet and various test networks), Filecoin, and IPFS. Off-chain applications can connect to Ethereum and IPFS via JSON-RPC over HTTPS and WebSocket, where request–response times are up to 20 times faster than other services and self-hosted solutions. Infura network nodes are running on the latest network upgrades with a minimum 99.9% uptime guarantee. The service is provided with per request or subscription-based connections and has full-time access to expert support teams.

A dashboard gives direct insights into the app's performance and API usage. This can be used to drill down into specific request methods or most active usage times to optimize the applications and better understand users.

Many leading blockchain-enabled products rely on Infura's services, for example, mobile applications (Coinbase Wallet), blockchain-compatible browsers and plug-ins (Brave, Metamask, Opera), and blockchain tools (OpenZeppelin, Truffle).

Infura is dominant, but a few alternate providers are active in this service area. ZMOK[54] provides fast Ethereum nodes accessible through JSON-RPC API. A similar service for the Ethereum network and the IPFS is available with the Cloudflare Distributed Web Gateway.[55] QuikNode[56] serves elastic APIs and dedicated nodes. Apart from Ethereum, their API endpoints include BSC, Optimism, Bitcoin, xDAI, and Polygon. Pocket Network[57] is an inclusive relay network for API requests to major blockchains with a crypto-economic model. The requests are routed to available nodes pseudo-randomly, making them very redundant. Compared to single-service providers, Pocket Network is organized as a decentralized autonomous organization (DAO). Its mission is to ensure the sustainable decentralization of blockchain infrastructure.

2.7.2.3 Public datasets for advanced blockchain data analytics

Ledger data derived directly from the network nodes might not have the most efficient structure for queries needed in the advanced BC data analyses, utilization of big data, machine learning, or business intelligence mechanisms. For this purpose, Google BigQuery, for example, provides public datasets to access the historical data from various BC networks, including access to the on-chain transaction data and entire block history. The data is, therefore, immediately available in all the analysis methods and visualization tools in BigQuery. In 2021, there were nearly 50 public datasets[58] available in the Google Cloud Platform marketplace. They include most key public blockchain networks, for example, BTC, Ethereum, Ethereum Classic,

---

53 https://infura.io/
54 https://zmok.io/
55 https://cloudflare-eth.com
56 https://www.quiknode.io
57 https://pokt.network
58 https://console.cloud.google.com/marketplace/browse?filter=solution-type:dataset&q=blockchain

Litecoin, Dash, Zcash, Monero, Cardano, NEO, etc. This data can be immediately applied in Google Cloud's AI services and data analytics or simply structured and queried with SQL.

The analysis can, for instance, reveal the most popular collectibles (ERC721 contracts) or tokens (ERC20 contracts), find zero-fee transactions, calculate balances of blockchain addresses, and so on.

3 Distributed ledgers and internet of things

Integration of distributed ledger technology and the Internet of Things is fundamental for many applications and use cases beyond decentralized finance (DeFi) applications. The application domains include, among others, smart cities, smart robotics, smart industry and logistics, mobility, and energy or waste management. Some of these application domains are discussed in more detail in Section 4.

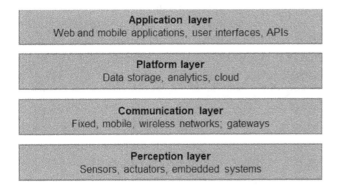

Fig. 3.1: Basic IoT architecture.

A basic cloud-centric IoT architecture is depicted in Fig. 3.1. The perception layer comprises sensors, actuators, and embedded devices that are integrated into things. The perception layer interacts with the real world, enables basic signal and data processing, and assures some form of connectivity (personal-area with Bluetooth or wired connections, local-area with WiFi, or wide-area with, e.g., Narrow-band IoT (NB-IoT)). The embedded device can thus attach directly or via a communication gateway to the communication layer, which is a public (Internet) or private IP network. The platform and the application layer are two sets of cloud-based services that enable the collection, storage, data processing, and the development of applications based on IoT data. Integration of IoT and DLT has long been seen as a remedy for the fundamental challenges of IoT architectures. The challenges, such as centralized ecosystems, cost of the connectivity, disrupted business models, security and trust, and lack of functional values, need to be addressed to continue with successful practical IoT deployments.

The great expectation imposed on the distributed ledger technology originated from the distributed and decentralized nature of DLT. For example, a decentralized approach to IoT networking was expected to solve many of the issues mentioned above. *"Blockchain technology is the missing link to cope with some of the future challenges in the IoT"* [46], which can reduce costs, build trust, accelerate transactions, provide scalability, remove single points of failure, keep an immutable record of the history of smart devices, enable machine-to-machine transactions, micropayments, and so on.

https://doi.org/10.1515/9783110681130-003

Unfortunately, many of these expectations were based on a simplified understanding of the technological and business-related scope of distributed ledger technology and unrealistic presumptions. For example, distributed ledger technology does not solve scalability problems of IoT. On the contrary, all relevant DLT deployments struggle to meet even a fraction of the capabilities (in terms of transactions per second and latency) of the current cloud-based IoT backend platforms. However, if the real benefits of the distributed ledger technology are understood, IoT DApps can be properly designed and carved, and the technology can be applied to situations where it can disrupt business operations. DLT opens vast opportunities for innovation and paradigm shifts in IoT [47]. Currently, we have production-grade systems capable of reliable IoT data collection or secure processing of tens of thousands of financial transactions. In most cases, the DLT struggles to meet the performance of centralized systems and is far from superseding them. Similarly, a single point of failure of a cloud application is merely a consequence of poor design and implementation. Cloud-based architectures leveraged by content distribution networks, platform virtualization, and application balancing and scaling can provide extremely reliable services. In 5 G networks, mechanisms for new service architectures are foreseen. A combination of cloud, edge, and mobile computing enables distributed (but not decentralized!) service deployment. Along with network-intrinsic resource assurance through network slices, they can support energy-efficient, massive, or time-sensitive IoT applications.

We see a meaningful role for DLT in IoT, not in alleviating the known IoT bottlenecks but in, predominantly, providing new features such as improved trust, full autonomy in device operation and business, seamless M2M transactions, and trusted operation through smart contracts, trustworthy DApps, data provenance, and fairness through financial incentives. Apart from the autonomous M2M communications via DApps, we see two other fundamental IoT and DLT integration concepts: data collection, and IoT device authentication, authorization, and (update) management. Both are presented in more detail further in this section.

Distributed ledger technology based IoT applications can be seen as a special case of DApps, where some additional requirements and limitations apply due to the nature of the IoT systems. These specifics are DL network performance, smart contract and end-device security (e.g., device access to the DL accounts), or implementation of the off-chain applications in constrained IoT devices. IoT solutions frequently impose industry-grade requirements on the underlying DL networks (see Section 2.3.2) and on the development and support ecosystems (see Section 2.7).

For the future successful decentralization of IoT, we need the integration of DL, IoT, and the underlying communication networks. In the traditional IoT architecture (Fig. 3.1), the IoT is considered merely an overlay on the communication infrastructure. The recent trends in 4 G already anticipate fog-/edge-based approaches, where some of the application and data logic is moved from the cloud into or closer to the IoT end-devices. In 5 G architectures, additional mechanisms (e.g., slicing) are foreseen to support the QoS or security in such a network architecture. Therefore, the next step in integration should be the organization and deployment of the appropriate DL network and DApp architecture to the fog, edge, and cloud-based communication infrastructure. Unlike DeFi applications, many of the IoT-related DApps do not require public or permissionless DL networks. This opens possibilities for novel DL network architectures, combining private, consortium, and public DL networks (see Section 2.3.1.1) implemented in the network edge or overlay services, and integrated by cross-chain swaps (Section 2.3.3.3).

3.1 Distributed ledgers for IoT security

Distributed ledger technology and blockchains, to a great degree, rely on advanced cybersecurity mechanisms and uniquely combine them to assure the trust expected from DLT systems. However, DLT does not simply improve all aspects of confidentiality, integrity, and availability of DL networks, systems, and applications. It does not come without its security risks (Table 3.1).

Confidentiality is not the key security feature that DLT was designed for. Sharing a common decentralized ledger among all network participants is essential to build decentralized trust. Unless very specific mechanisms and DL network architectures are applied, DL data is transparent, and DL network users are at most pseudo-anonymous.

Integrity is a security feature that DLT was invented for. It refers to the immutability of transactions, tamper-proof deployment, and execution of smart contract code. However, these same features open new privacy and security risks, even leading to unprecedented legal or ethical issues in the use of DLT applications and systems.

Availability of a system tends to improve if the system is distributed and decentralized. Despite no single central point to be attacked in a DL network, DLT systems are not immune to denial of service or other attacks that impact availability. The attacks target the DL network services, consensus processes, or decentralized applications. The denial might affect only selected network nodes or network participants. Besides the DL network, there are few decentralized entities in the system that are prone to traditional distributed denial of service (DDoS) attacks. These attacks limit the availability of, for example, oracles and API servers or off-chain and auxiliary services such as crypto exchanges and mining pools.

Various vectors frequently converge onto one attack area. The first objective is to gain control over the network, a part of the network, or individual nodes, and then exploit this control to manipulate transactions and impact integrity. Some of the attack vectors might be extremely hard and costly to execute. In a truly decentralized DL network, they might almost be practically infeasible. However, in more centralized, private or consensus networks, the risks remain real.

Despite some security limitations highlighted in this section, the trusted nature of distributed ledger technology systems enables further security enhancements in IoT systems [47]. These range from data management and integrity to confidentiality

Tab. 3.1: Confidentiality, integrity, and availability aspects of blockchain technologies for IoT.

	Aspects
Confidentiality	– Blockchain data is not confidential, by default.
	– Pseudo anonymity in public networks.
	– Private and consortium networks improve confidentiality.
	– Zero-knowledge mechanisms for privacy.
Integrity	– Integrity is where DLT shines.
	– Yet, risks are present. Transaction tampering usually occurs after a node or network participant has been denied trusted access to DL network services.
	– The immutability of DLT transactions and smart contracts imposes relevant new security and privacy risks.
Availability	– Distributed nature of DLT increases the availability of the on-chain data and services, compared to consolidated solutions.
	– New attack vectors can impair network availability.

and PKI management, with a decentralized backend and decentralized methods for authentication and authorization of IoT devices and users.

3.1.1 Confidentiality and privacy

A shared ledger is a common truth that assures trust in the distributed ledger technology system. In public blockchain networks, access to the ledger is not at all limited. Anyone can access, read, and redistribute the content of the ledger, including all transactions. Everyone can analyze every detail of each past transaction in a blockchain network. In public networks, users do not have to present any personal identity to create a new blockchain account. This keeps them private as persons, but the account activities, including the cryptocurrency balance, are public. Public DL networks are, therefore, pseudo-anonymous. Frequently, for regulatory reasons, personal identity must be verified when users create an account in crypto exchanges. This links their personal identity to their public blockchain accounts and discards their anonymity and privacy.

In permissioned networks, only the authenticated nodes have access to the ledger. Access to the ledger is not public anymore, but is limited to known network participants. This is very favorable for business-related blockchain systems, for example, industrial IoT, smart grid, etc. Apart from this, there is usually no other leger access control. Permissioned networks enhance the privacy of interactions by excluding anonymous public, but still do not enable confidentiality and privacy that are known in a traditional online application.

User content in transactions (e.g., data filed in an Ethereum transaction) can be encrypted. This can be end-to-end encryption, which is not an intrinsic feature of the DL network protocols, but implemented in off-chain applications. In this case, the blockchain transactions are utilized as a transport mechanism for encrypted content and decrypted out-of-chain. This approach enhances the confidentiality of user data in transactions but limits the use of user data in smart contracts.

Besides, information about users and usage patterns can be disclosed from blockchain transaction traffic too. We can carry out big data analysis of the publicly available chain data to reveal important account and DApp usage patterns. These approaches are being used to analyze transaction linkability, transaction mixing, crypto laundering, and smart contract use, impacting user privacy.

One direction of blockchain research [48] aims to provide zero-knowledge proofs, which reveal nothing about a transaction, except that it is valid, to increase privacy in blockchains. Through complex cryptographic methods, zero-knowledge proof can prove something is true without having to reveal what exactly it is proving. One of the first examples was ZK-SNARK, used in Zcash. Apart from zero-knowledge proofs, zero-knowledge methods have been used as a baseline to enable privacy preservation in blockchain, including secure multi-party computation, commitment schemes, ZK-SNARK, ZK-STARK, ring signatures, and homomorphic hiding. ZK-SNARKs require a trusted party or parties to set up the zero-knowledge proof system, initially. These trusted parties can violate the privacy of the entire system. ZK-STARKs improve upon this technology by removing the need for a trusted setup. Integration of ZK-STARK is being considered as one of the possible features in Ethereum 2.0.

3.1.2 Availability

Distributed ledger network attacks are usually the basis for further attacks that impact integrity. They target the governance or operation of a DL network, with the objective of taking control of most nodes and thus, the entire ledger (e.g., 51% attack). Network attacks might also try to partition the DL network into several separate and inconsistent partitions or isolate a selected node from the remaining trusted nodes (Eclipse attack, Sybil).

This is then followed by presenting the node under attack with a deceptive state of the ledger, often by manipulating the node's time perception under attack (e.g., Timejacking, Delay attack).

Mining nodes and consensus mechanisms are vulnerable too. A mining node can be dishonest and behave selfishly and withhold some of the already mined blocks (e.g., Selfish mining, Block withholding). In this manner, miners attempt to increase their share of the reward. Effective countermeasures include the application of block timers or increasing the randomness of the miner pool assignments.

3.2 Data management

Although blockchains are distributed databases, public blockchain networks cannot directly meet the back-end database replacement requirements in IoT systems. The transaction structure is optimized for blockchain operation. With distributed consensus, new entries are added to storage to assure the distributed nature, immutability, and the absence of central authorities. However, it cannot meet the high throughput, low latency, rich permissioning, or query capabilities of traditional or distributed databases [47].

Some of the blockchain protocols facilitate the placement of additional data in a transaction. These can be parameters in a smart contract call or even arbitrary data, for example, a JSON input filed in an Ethereum transaction. However, extensive data included in transactions would result in extensive chain data and costs for storing data in the chain.

IoT applications generate large volumes of traffic and are often latency-sensitive. Therefore, it is not surprising that most blockchain-based IoT data management approaches such as IPFS, FairAccess, ENIGMA, or BigchainDB, take a hybrid approach. These combine off-chain storage and blockchain capabilities with management functions assigned to the blockchain to ensure integrity and transparency, in applications that require auditable records. Only smaller pieces of information are stored in the chain, such as hash values of the off-chain data or access control information. Despite off-loading a large part of traffic from the blockchain networks, these approaches still need to provide lower latency and higher throughput record-keeping than public blockchain networks; so, private or consortium blockchains are used.

BigchainDB,[59] for example, starts with a big data distributed database and then adds blockchain characteristics such as decentralized control via a federation of voting, immutability, and transfer of digital assets. Once stored, data cannot be changed or deleted. At the same time, it facilitates any MongoDB query to search the contents of all stored transactions, assets, metadata, and blocks.

As shown in Fig. 3.2, BigchainDB can be seamlessly integrated into the traditional application stack as a blockchain database for decentralized timestamping, certificates, smart contracts, and transactions. At the same time, it can be part of a fully decentralized application, where processing and file storage are decentralized.

They took a hybrid approach in an integrated IoT blockchain platform for sensing data integrity [49], where large files are stored in separate off-chain databases. The system utilizes a private permissioned Hyperledger Fabric blockchain network, along with a dedicated IoT server, for key device and user services. Application logic in the system is thus partly implemented with traditional approaches and partly as smart contracts. The system enables users' registration and device enrolment, where certificates are

---

59 https://www.bigchaindb.com

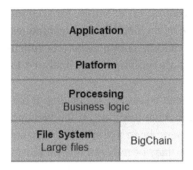 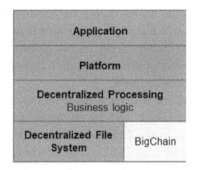

Fig. 3.2: Reference stack for the BigchainDB applications – traditional and decentralized application stacks.

granted to the communicating entities to authenticate their transactions. It provides an immutable log of device data and allows easy access to the deployed devices.

3.3 Authentication and authorization

Authentication and authorization are two fundamental steps in any ICT system to manage access by various entities such as the users, devices, and services. They are based on unique entity identifiers, sets of mechanisms to authenticate the identity of a particular entity, and rules to authorize the collection of predefined rights and services in the system.

In the IoT, the common identification, authentication, and authorization approaches need to be adapted to avoid single-point failures in complex and large-scale IoT network infrastructures and simplify enrolment and authentication for constrained, unmanned devices.

Blockchain technologies can contribute to device identification, for example, by granting unique blockchain addresses to devices for authentication and authorization. Based on smart contract capabilities in the blockchain, the latter verifies their identity and grants the appropriate rights. An additional benefit of the blockchain-based approach is the transparent and immutable history of authentication and authorization actions.

3.3.1 Identification and device enrolment

For authentication and authorization, users, devices, and services in any ICT system need unique and distinguishable identities. For devices, this can be in the form of a hardware address assigned by the manufacturer (e.g., Media Access-Control address for Ethernet or Bluetooth devices and IMEI for mobile devices) or an identifier that is granted to the device during the enrolment procedure, for example, an account address, token or a blockchain account. Some of the novel identification techniques rely on device fingerprinting. In this approach, a device does not possess an explicit identifier. Instead, devices' communication patterns are monitored and analyzed to identify a device uniquely.

In the IoT, the enrolment phase for new devices can be rather challenging. It has to be reliable, secure, and yet minimize or even eliminate any human intervention during the enrolment. This is especially critical, for example, in massive deployments of unmanned devices. The backend for the enrolment may or may not rely on blockchain technology. In IoT systems that are not based on hardware identifiers, the device owner usually executes the enrolment. If, for example, a blockchain address is used to identify a device, it is assigned manually. Often, details about wallet control in the device are not clearly explained. This can lead to relevant hardware security risks, similar to those related to PKI private key management. It is, therefore, not surprising that many blockchain-based IoT systems predominantly focus on authentication and authorization of users and services.

An approach toward a simplified and, to a large extent, automated enrolment of IoT devices, where a device is granted a unique blockchain-based address for identification, could mimic, for example, the Easy Connect approach to manage network access in WPA3. It simplifies device configuration by using QR codes, NFC tags, downloaded device information from the cloud, or a user-chosen configurator such as a smartphone. A result of a blockchain-based adaption of this onboarding procedure would be a unique blockchain address registered in the backend system and assigned to the device for consequent authorization.

For users and services, known identification principles can be adapted to leverage blockchain technology in the backend. Self-sovereign identity (SSI) is an emerging approach for establishing digital identity based on decentralized technologies. Unlike the centralized identity paradigm where some central trusted issuer provides identities, SSI users control the scope and use of their verifiable information. SSI is user-centric and privacy-aware, and reduces the unintended sharing of personal data. In an SSI system, entities are identified by decentralized identifiers (DID). The trust and management of DIDs are assured by blockchain technology, and DIDs can be decoupled from centralized registries, identity providers, and certificate authorities. Although the initial motivation for SSI was to increase the security and privacy of digital citizens, the same framework can be adapted for non-person subjects and, thus, for IoT [50] too. Anything can be a DID subject: a person, group, an organization, a material thing, a digital thing, a logical thing, etc.

3.3.2 Authentication

When a unique blockchain address has been assigned and used to identify devices, the authenticity can be verified for every transaction created by a particular device. If a device has access to the blockchain account associated with the given blockchain address, it can create valid transactions. A verifiable transaction origin is the basic trust feature of a blockchain system. So, if a transaction originates from a correct device address and the transaction is valid (not rejected during block creation), we can assume that it was created by the authentic device and not by some other device claiming the same identity.

If authentication is needed to access some on-chain smart contract capabilities, the access authorization can rely solely on such authentication. In Ethereum smart contracts, for example, there is a tx.origin global variable in Solidity that returns the account's address that sent the transaction. However, the authentication based on tx. origin can be exposed to a transaction origin attack, a form of a phishing attack. Therefore, tx.origin authentication in smart contracts is usually combined with the msg. sender variable, which identifies the sending smart contract and not the originating account. For details, see Section 2.4.4.2.4.

A blockchain system can also be used only as an underlying technology to authenticate and authorize devices for access control in an off-chain service. In this case, the purpose of the decentralized application is to securely grant a device, a user, or a backend system, the appropriate identification and authentication information, such as a token, one-time password, IP address, or a certificate. This information is then used to authenticate a given entity and to manage the service access. Apart from identification and authentication information, in this way, we can issue the entities some initial authorization data or credentials too. Here, blockchain-based identification and authentication of devices are primarily not about access to the smart contract method, but about access to other entities in the IoT architecture.

Strict access control requires the authentic identity of the communicating devices. In IoT, a dedicated gateway frequently manages the identities, which are then used when authenticating with others [51]. The forms of these identities are very diverse, including, for example, unique virtual IPv6 addresses, one-time passwords, unforgeable tokens, or other credentials.

3.3.3 Authorization and access control

Traditional access control technologies govern the ability of users and devices to access capabilities and services made available by entities of the same kind. The OM-AM reference model can help us define the organizational security and access control policy in a heterogeneous environment. This is a four-layer model, where each layer is designed separately. Horizontally, within each layer, we can compare the alternative access control aspects. Vertically, we compare and combine different access control policies. The reference model is depicted in Fig. 3.3. OM-AM stands for Objective, Model, Architecture, and Mechanism. The objective and model (OM) layers articulate what the security objectives are and what should be achieved, while the architecture and mechanism (AM) layers address how to meet those requirements [52].

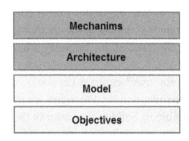

Fig. 3.3: Authorization reference model for IoT.

3.3.3.1 Authorization models

The possible access control models differ in many aspects, including granularity, flexibility, centralization, and interoperability. They are, therefore, not equally appropriate for implementation in IoT systems. In Sections 3.3.1 and 3.3.2, we highlight some possible approaches for identifying and authentication IoT devices with DLT. Nevertheless, the decentralized approach is merely one option and device identification can be managed in the traditional (centralized) way. Similarly, access control can utilize centralized or decentralized approaches.

Identity-based access control (IBAC) is a type of security that focuses on access to digital information or services based on the authenticated identity of an entity. Discretionary access control (DAC) considers the authenticated identity and the groups to which the entities belong. In DAC, subjects can transfer access controls among each other. Therefore, the name is discretionary. With a huge number of devices, IBAC and DAC become unsuitable for IoT because it is almost impossible to manage the appropriate access control lists for everyone in the system.

On the other hand, in mandatory access control (MAC), the security policy is centrally controlled by a security policy administrator. Users cannot override or modify this policy – therefore, mandatory. A risk with MAC is high centralization and a single-point failure in the controller. IoT devices at diverse locations or with different functions may belong to various management organizations. This imposes another relevant problem for the centralized mandatory access control model, which does not fit IoT systems.

We can simultaneously implement MAC and DAC, where DAC refers to one category of access controls that entities can transfer among each other. MAC refers to the second category of access controls that imposes constraints upon the first.

Role-based access control (RBAC) employs pre-defined roles that carry a specific set of privileges. It can enforce MAC and DAC access control models too. Despite being used to manage access control in large organizations with hundreds of users and thousands of permissions, RBAC might not be flexible and scalable enough for IoT.

Attribute-based access control (ABAC), also known as policy-based access control, is more flexible and scalable, dynamic, and can provide a more fine-grained access control that is needed in IoT. There are no access lists or roles in the system. Instead, attributes are assigned to every device, and only those with enough attributes that match the access policy are allowed. The policies can express a complex Boolean rule set and can evaluate many different attributes. In several examples, DLT was applied to record the distribution of attributes in ABAC. In [51], a simplified DLT-based access control protocol suitable for IoT is proposed.

Most traditional access control models face a common problem –a credible center is needed to ensure trust. Besides, in [52], they presented an extensive review of various access control schemes for IoT. The conclusion is that traditional access control mechanisms may not be completely appropriate for resource-constrained environments.

3.3.3.2 OAuth authorization architecture

The OAuth 2.0 [53] is a commonly applied authorization framework, which introduces an authorization layer and separates the role of the client from that of the resource owner. This standardized protocol provides specific authorization flows (Fig. 3.4) for web or desktop applications, mobile devices, applications, or IoT, and simplifies the overall authorization architecture and client development. In OAuth, the client requests access to resources controlled by the resource owner and hosted by the resource server, and is issued a set of credentials different from those of the resource owner.

Instead of using the resource owner's credentials to access protected resources, the client obtains an access token – a string denoting a specific scope, lifetime, and other access attributes. Access tokens are issued to third-party clients by an authorization server with the approval of the resource owner. OAuth does not pass authentication data between clients and resource providers, but instead acts as an authorization token. The client uses the access token to access the protected resources hosted by the resource server. However, [54] showed that to run all OAuth logic in a resource-constrained device might be impossible because of its high communication and computation overheads.

3.3.3.3 Decentralized authorization examples

FairAccess [55] was an early attempt at a decentralized authorization management framework for IoT using blockchain. As one of the first, it pointed out the need for granularity, privacy, transparency, and sovereignty in identification and authentication. The implementation reflects the infant times of blockchain technologies. In FairAccess, they use the UTXO model of blockchain and BTC-like addresses to identify all interacting entities. The underlying blockchain network supported no smart

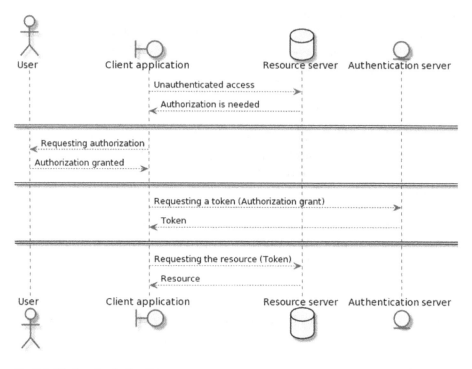

Fig. 3.4: OAuth authorization flow.

contracts as we know them today. It uses new types of transactions to grant, get, delegate, or revoke access to users. Scripting language to express fine-grained and contextual access control policies is enveloped inside these transactions. An access token is required to obtain access to a protected resource. A transaction does not deliver the access token until the requester fulfills all access control conditions already described with the model and included in the transaction. As a proof of concept of this idea, two access control models (identity and permissioned access control models) have been used in the implementation.

As OAuth is dependent on a trusted third-party authentication provider, which has total control over user data, an authentication server could block certain applications and thus deny the services provided by the application. DAuth [56] provides an OAuth-like authentication service based on the Ethereum blockchain. A decentralized approach provides trustless architecture, and enhances transparency and user control. In DAuth, resource owners (users) are registered with their blockchain addresses in the authentication smart contract. For authorization, the backend application requests the user's blockchain address from the smart contract and, at the same time, asks the user to sign an authentication request message with the same blockchain account credentials. It then compares the signatures of the user and the smart contract. If they match, the application provides resources to the user.

VaultPoint [57] is a new blockchain-based self-sovereign identity management model that complies with the popular and mature standard of OAuth 2.0. It follows the authorization code grant type of OAuth, which comprises the client authorization, user authentication, and issuance of access tokens. The proposed model could make Web or mobile development easy and reduce users' burden of learning new authentication and authorization processes, because they are already familiar with OAuth. Using blockchain, the proposed model provides decentralization and integrity of the user and client information, and guarantees the reliability of the authentication and authorization processes. The system is based on the Ethereum blockchain. Three types of smart contracts are used – identification, notification, and client management contract. The proposed model not only solves the information centralization and the privacy issue of the existing federated ID management models governed by major companies, but it also provides users with secure accessibility to and sovereignty over their information.

3.4 Monetization

Distributed ledger technology can successfully keep trusted records of monetary transactions. If this aspect of distributed ledger technology is integrated with IoT, it enables development of new business models. IoT ecosystems can be extremely heterogeneous in their applications, technologies, and involved stakeholders. A decentralized ecosystem business model, for example, in a smart city, can prioritize the overall benefits of the entire community and the greater ecosystem objectives, instead of maximizing fragmented values such as the profit of the involved individual participants [58].

The IoT business market is multi-faceted. Different entities involved in the ecosystem can serve multiple sides of the market and play various roles in the business model. Multi-faced roles of the participants not only affect the business model, they directly impose authentication and authorization in the system, supported by the decentralized approaches. Refer Section 3.3. In an illustrative example in Section 3.6, we demonstrate, to some extent, such a multi-faced stakeholder environment. For example, each participating autonomous machine can act as a service provider or a service consumer.

Several vendors are involved in IoT ecosystem provisioning, including software and hardware vendors, communication and information service providers, and solution providers. They need compensation for their investments into IoT infrastructures, as well as for service provisioning. Monetization of data plays a key role in the IoT ecosystem, in data ownership and sharing. The data generated by the IoT devices are usually accompanied by rich contextual information, which can be monetized, too. However, this requires efficient and granular control over data. Two business models are prominent in data monetization. First, where the data owner offers their data in exchange for services provided by a third-party provider, and second, where the owner pays to keep his data protected while using the same services.

Monetary and non-monetary aspects of the distributed ledger technology can be combined in the same decentralized IoT solution. However, this opens new issues related to the DL network architectures and their interoperability for diverse application requirements. Networks with seemingly similar technological backgrounds may strongly differ in practical implementation, governance, and performance. In decentralized monetization of IoT, one enforces a public, permissionless network for user interfaces. In the other, a permissioned consortium network meets the machine interfaces' performance requirements and reduces the transaction costs.

3.5 Integration schemes of internet of things and the distributed ledger

Embedded IoT devices are often characterized by low power consumption for prolonged battery autonomy and are prone to stringent production cost containment because of their mass scale. This limits the computation and storage capabilities of IoT devices and their cryptographic capabilities. For energy efficiency in IoT, WAN (e.g., LoRaWAN, NB-IoT) or PAN (e.g., Bluetooth), wireless communication technologies are optimized for low power operation too. IoT devices are, therefore, not used as full blockchain nodes, because the computation and communication overheads do not justify the potential benefits or because a full blockchain node is simply impossible to be implemented in a constrained device [47].

The processing power of a constrained device impedes the use of advanced encryption protocols and limits the blockchain functions that a constrained device can execute. Limited storage makes it impossible to keep the entire chain data or even all block headers in an IoT device.

The communication traffic of a blockchain network node consists of a continuous traffic needed for synchronization with the blockchain network and a sporadic traffic due to transaction submission and event notification. The continuous traffic results from the DL network operation and is not affected by the DApp design and implementation. The only way to alleviate continuous traffic from the IoT device is to withdraw blockchain synchronization protocols and allocate them to a more capable edge gateway. The sporadic traffic is application dependent and can be, at least to some extent, limited by appropriate DApp workflow design. It occurs only when the device-machine interface (MI) submits a new transaction to the network for confirmation or when a device receives an event notification for MI applications in the device, to react to state changes in smart contracts.

Limited user interactions with IoT devices, for example, in unmanned devices without user interfaces, inhibit flexible and secure management of blockchain credentials needed for security and identification. This impacts device enrolment and authentication procedures.

Absolute decentralization in IoT is, therefore, problematic. We may adjust blockchain network architectures and protocols and the designs of IoT DApps and IoT machine interfaces to cope with the IoT device constraints, and assure the needed network performance and latency.

3.5.1 Distributed ledger networks for internet of things

Distributed ledger networks are discussed in detail in Section 2.3. In IoT, we try to attune performance, scalability, network costs, and privacy. The requirement imposed by IoT devices on a DL network might be different from that of a DeFi application. If such divergent application aspects need to be combined in the same decentralized application, both the public and consortium networks (Section 2.3.3.3) can be applied and cross-chained (Section 2.3.3.3). In public networks, other consensus algorithms from PoW can be used such as PoS or PoA (Section 2.3.2.1) to reduce transaction costs and improve performance. In private or consortium networks for IoT, a simplified version of the PoW consensus can be found. However, this reduces the decentralization and the inherent trust. Some of the distributed ledger technologies try to combine the financial and IoT performance (and privacy) aspects in one network (e.g., IOTA).

3.5.2 Internet of things device architectures for DApps

Table 3.2 summarizes the levels of involvement in the blockchain protocol execution of various entities, that is, network nodes and IoT devices. IoT devices usually act as transaction issuers or requesters. The full or light nodes are not IoT end-devices but dedicated entities that provide blockchain network capabilities. We can split blockchain functions (e.g., chain synchronization, event filtering, transaction creation, validation, or key-store management) between the IoT devices, edge gateways, and full blockchain network nodes. Then, we adapt the off-chain application logic to IoT device, accordingly [25]. A common approach is that the IoT device only creates and signs its transactions; the gateway performs all other blockchain operations, which serves as a light network node and manages the entire communication with the blockchain network. Even a less demanding option is an IoT device without any capabilities, and a gateway, which runs all blockchain functions, including transaction creation and signing.

An IoT device that is a transaction issuer is capable of building and signing a valid blockchain transaction. The issuer has a valid blockchain identity. It needs access to the key-store to properly sign the issued transaction. Access to the key store requires reliable authentication in the device and can impose hardware security risks. After a transaction is built, it is submitted to the blockchain network via an API in one of the network nodes.

Tab. 3.2: Types of IoT blockchain entities.

	Storage	Validator	Account keys
Full Node	Full chain data	Yes	Yes
Light Node	Block headers	No	Yes
Transaction Issuer	None	No	Yes
Transaction Requester	None	No	No

In the architecture of a constrained Ethereum-based IoT device, depicted in Fig. 3.5, we see the approach where the blockchain client is installed on a separate, unconstrained edge gateway. This gateway is capable of running all blockchain protocols as a full or as a light client. The device is attached to the DL client API to avail the DL functions provided by the gateway. The architecture in this figure assumes that the device can securely keep its key-store. The device is also capable enough to build and sign transactions and communicate through the DL client API with the DL edge gateway/node.

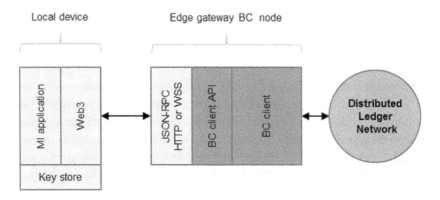

Fig. 3.5: IoT transaction issuer device and edge gateway Ethereum node.

A transaction requester is a pure IoT device. It runs only the traditional IoT protocols and has no access to the blockchain key-store. It cannot directly take any of the blockchain-specific actions and runs no blockchain protocols. A transaction requester only assembles data for submission, communicates it with a network node, which then issues the transaction on its behalf. Thus, the transaction requester relies on a gateway device, which integrates the traditional IoT protocol principles with a blockchain operation.

In Fig. 3.6, the IoT device's off-chain logic communicates with the edge gateway through a proprietary communication interface, which is in no way related to DL.

The device also possesses no DL-related credentials. All functions, including the DL transaction creation, are done in the application logic of the edge gateway, where the key-store is also kept. This can vastly reduce the requirements imposed on the device. However, the IoT device does not directly benefit now from any decentralized trust enhancements and must fully trust the edge gateway.

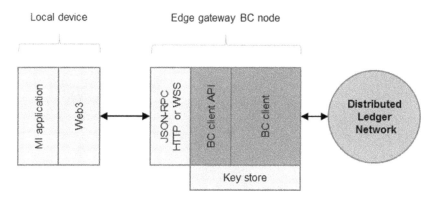

Fig. 3.6: IoT transaction requester device and edge gateway Ethereum node.

These architectural arrangements help us in coping with the IoT device communication and computation constraints and are often the only viable approaches to include a constrained IoT device in decentralized applications. However, we need to be aware that this reduces the decentralization of the system. Therefore, a possible unfavorable impact on overall trust may not be neglected.

3.6 Example of an industrial internet of things DApp

The Tetramax technology transfer experiment CORONA[60] combines distributed ledger technology with collaborative robotics. This proof of concept enables innovative IoT machine autonomy use cases in manufacturing environments, such as servitization and robotics-as-a-service. As an illustrative example, a 3-D printer can offer its printing capabilities to other actors in the system. Machines or other actors can place an order for such a service. The service negotiation is then autonomously conducted through blockchain transactions and smart contracts. The printing machine records the process of production. This is used as a confirmation of the work done and is recorded in the blockchain. The basic use case diagram is depicted in Fig. 3.7.

The actors have unique blockchain accounts and are identified by blockchain addresses. The business logic for the activities in the use cases is implemented in smart

---

60 https://ltfe.org/en/portfolio/corona/

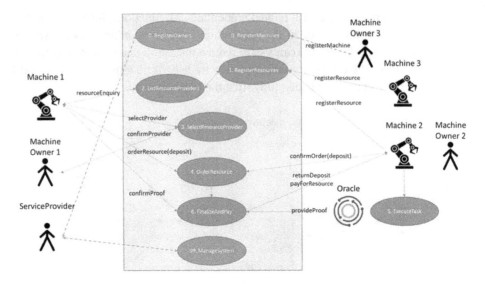

Fig. 3.7: Use-case diagram of a decentralized collaborative robotic system.

contracts and executed through machine and user interfaces. The machines interface the blockchain system through the applications in single-board computers. Trusted machines are oracles that provide data to smart contracts from the external world.

The entire communication between the machines includes placing, confirming, and executing an order. If the task is finalized on time and the required proof of execution is provided, the order is completed. A key message exchange in the system for placing and executing an order is shown in Fig. 3.8.

The data and event model is based on a UML class diagram, modified to include the smart contract methods and parameters, and the events thrown up during operation. Therefore, the required system data was split into three categories: obligatory, auxiliary, and large or binary objects. The key items are implemented as smart contract parameters. These are the obligatory parameters for minimum system functionality; for example, order IDs or machine addresses. Some additional parameters are placed in the transaction data field as a JSON string. They, too, are kept in the blockchain, but their structure can be adapted without directly affecting the smart contract code. This allows for some flexibility; for example, adding new parameter fields to a description of a machine or a user. The large or binary objects, for example, printer configuration files, image and video proofs of manufacturing, etc., are not kept in the blockchain because of their size. Instead, they are placed on the off-chain storage servers, and only their hash values are set in the chain.

The solution is a decentralized application, which is based on Ethereum technology. A Proof of Authority consortium-based blockchain network was set up to overcome some of the performance and cost limitations of blockchain and IoT. Block time was set to 3 s, which is substantially less than in, for example, a public Ethereum

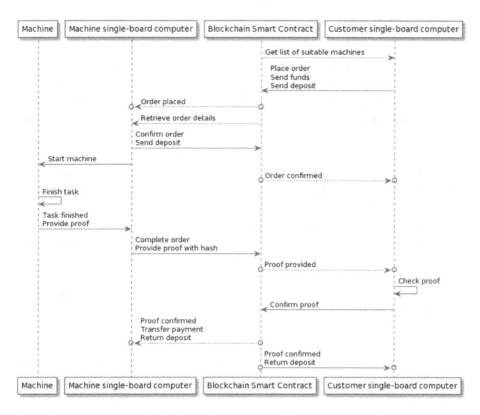

Fig. 3.8: Message sequence for placing and executing an order.

network. This allows for better transaction throughput and lower latency. Besides, the PoA mechanism provides very predictable block times and is not energy-consuming. The network runs the smart contract platform. The UI and MI access the blockchain capabilities through the access nodes that are HTTP RPC enabled.

Smart contract platform enables back-end logic for registering new machines and machine owners, selecting the appropriate service providers, and placing and managing the orders. All interactions with the smart contract are role-based, and a role is defined for a selected blockchain account. This enables secure execution of the entire smart contract functionality.

The user interface enables the configuration and monitoring of the system. It is used to register and configure details about machine owners, register new machines, and monitor events related to the order execution. The general Web technologies (HTML, JavaScript, Vue) and interfaces hide the blockchain specifics and details from the user. However, the UI Web application is blockchain aware and only operates if the user has the required access credentials and is authenticated by the appropriate blockchain account.

4 Selected use cases

These days, cryptocurrencies are certainly the most popular use cases of distributed ledger technologies, with Bitcoin as the first one that made a breakthrough in this area. Over the years, in its initial design, blockchain technology was used in several applications in both financial and non-financial domains where, in the past, third party trusted entities for transactions' verification and protection was necessary.

In addition to blockchain, the smart contracts application (invented in 1994) for the automatic execution of contracts between involved parties was enforced by computer protocols. And yet, smart contracts did not come into use until blockchain technology enabled their easy registration, verification, and execution, that is, until programmable payments became a reality. Now, smart contracts, supported by blockchain or other distributed ledger technologies (e.g., hashgraph), that ensure payments are triggered when the preprogrammed conditions of the contract agreements are met, represent the cutting edge of the cryptocurrency world. The combination of smart contracts and distributed ledger technology enables many decentralized applications, while Bitcoin and other cryptocurrencies make up only a small part of the DLT ecosystem.

Generally speaking, a smart contract is the computer code whose execution enables exchanging anything that has value (money, shares, property, content, etc.). It is a self-operating program running on a DLT platform (e.g., on the Ethereum blockchain) that executes automatically when specific conditions are met. Due to the execution on a DLT platform, a smart contract runs exactly as programmed (according to the agreed contract terms), that is, there is no chance of it being changed, interrupted, censored, or interfered by any third party.

Regarding physical hardware, the smart contract code is executed on every network node of the platform. In the case of a blockchain-supported smart contract, the execution of the smart contract code is part of the definition of the state transition function within the block validation algorithm. For example, if a transaction is part of a block that is to be validated, the code assigned to that transaction will be executed on all nodes, validating the given block.

Smart contracts can be used in many cases, that is, they can replace arrangements in which some assets must be transferred only when certain conditions are met. These conditions require lawyers (for contract creation) and banks (for providing escrow service). There are also other numerous DApps in their development that can be used in various sectors and not only in financial ones. Some areas where DLT-based applications are (or might be) used are listed below, by category.

Financial sector:
- Money and payments (cryptocurrencies and sub-currencies, payment authorization, clearance, cross-border payments, micropayments, foreign exchange)

https://doi.org/10.1515/9783110681130-004

- Ownership and collateral registries (land registries, property titles registries, movable asset registries)
- Financial services (notarization services and mortgages, syndicated loans, automated insurance pay-outs and validation of occurrence of an insured event, crowdfunding, commodities trading, trading of securities, wills, hedging contracts, savings wallets).

Other sectors:
- Governance (E-Residence, E-voting systems, record-keeping – e.g., criminal records, protection against cyberattacks)
- Healthcare (E-Medical records)
- Automotive industry (autonomous driving systems improvements, car locking/unlocking, electric car charge payment, parking, and other payments)
- Agriculture (agricultural insurance, safety net programs related to delivery of seeds and fertilizers, crop finance, and warehouse receipts)
- Trade and commerce (invoice management, supply-chain tracking, and management, intellectual property registration, product authenticity, Internet of Things)
- Humanitarian (tracking distribution and expenditure of aid money, tracking delivery and distribution of food, vaccinations, medications, etc.)
- Identity and reputation systems (name registration systems, DNS, e-mail authentication, SSI)
- Data (decentralized file storage)
- Decentralized Autonomous Organizations
- Prediction markets, peer-to-peer gambling

The spectrum of the possible use cases that involve distributed ledger technologies is very broad. Next, provided are some concrete examples, emphasizing some issues related to the car industry, smart mobility, and smart energy.

4.1 Car industry 4.0

In Section 4.1, some possible DLT use cases related to car industry will be described/proposed. It is also expected that DLTs will be much more integrated with future smart cars and involved in their production. DLT is anticipated to play a significant role in the rollout of Industry 4.0 [59] in general, and particularly as part of Car Industry 4.0.

Today's car industry faces numerous challenges and changes due to many factors such as climate changes, new regulations, security and safety challenges of car-to-car and Car-to-Infrastructure communication, new hardware and software architecture, new functionalities, and new business models. As an answer to all these factors, several disruptive technologies have come into focus.

The introduction of the concept of Industry 4.0 has a dramatic impact in many areas, and the car manufacturing industry is not an exception. The term Industry 4.0 refers to the fourth industrial revolution, but it is not yet completely defined. It rather denotes a set of emerging technologies and tools with the potential to drastically improve various manufacturing processes. More specifically, under the concept of Industry 4.0, a synergy between the traditional industrial processes and digitalization is assumed. The achieved manufacturing solutions are performed by the intelligent networking of machines and processes in the industry with the help of information and communication technology [59]. Industry 4.0 is also known as Smart Manufacturing, which offers solutions involving one or more technologies:

- Internet of Things (IoT)
- Artificial Intelligence (AI)
- Augmented Reality (AR)
- Automation/Robotics
- Additive manufacturing/3D printing
- Machine-to-machine communication (M2M)

Distributed ledger technology is also a technological group that can be added to the earlier list of Industry 4.0 pillars.

Similar to the term Industry 4.0, the term smart car does not precisely determine the requirements that a car must meet to be considered smart. In the past, this term denoted a car with advanced electronics enabling some useful enhancements as reverse and blind-spot sensing, GPS navigation, or assisted parking, for example. These enhancements may also include voice control, tire pressure monitoring, systems for keeping a safe distance from other cars and objects, Internet connection, etc.

In a stricter sense, a smart car has numerous enhancements and ability to be highly interconnected (e.g., via WiFi, Bluetooth, 4 G/5 G) and possesses a certain level of self-driving automation capabilities (from assisted driving to fully autonomous driving).

Usage of the IoT technology in the future is indispensable, as IoT assumes implementation of sensors of all types, sensor data collection, and transfer to data processing units via wireless communication. IoT is an enabler of numerous car-related applications, including car-to-car (C2C) communication, or the communication between cars and other objects, that is, vehicle-to-environment (V2E), vehicle-to-infrastructure (V2I) communication, etc. [60].

An implication of the fast expansion of artificial intelligence (AI) over the last decade is that AI-based solutions are increasingly deployed in the cars' autonomous driving systems. One typical example is avoiding sudden obstacles or incidents that may appear during autonomous driving. For that purpose, an artificial neural network (ANN) [61] implemented within a separate computer unit of a car can be trained based on the driving data collected when the car is driven in different environmental conditions. This training is performed for a longer period on different types of roads where various unexpected obstacles appear from time to time. Unfortunately, avoiding obstacles and surprises on the road still cannot be solved using standard systems of autonomous driving (radar, LIDAR [62], GPS, and different signal processing techniques). A well-trained ANN is expected to recognize almost all dangerous situations on the road that may happen during a real drive and act at the right time to avoid these situations. Additionally, the driving should be comfortable, assuming the absence of sudden braking, accelerations, or sharp direction changes (except in cases where a sharp direction change cannot be avoided). The most important trump card of autonomous driving is that safety and driving efficiency will be better than when a typical (average) human drives, and this goal has already been achieved in many situations. ANN training is similar to (but much shorter than) the process of teaching (or training) a person to drive. Additionally, once trained, the ANN can be implemented to all cars of the same model, without the necessity of training each car's ANN separately [63].

Unlike virtual reality (VR) where a person is in a completely different reality due to reproducing specific visual content through dark VR glasses and specific audio content in headphones, augmented reality (AR) does not replace a person's reality but rather enriches it by the additional useful information that can be implemented either by the use of projectors mounted in the working environment or by glasses projecting the additional content in one part of the visual field. Like the vizor of a fighter pilot, various guidance lines, markers, arrows, warning signs, etc., are projected to help the driver. Typical examples are drawing the road edges in cases of poor visibility, displaying critical alert signs on the front glass, and helping the driver by various warning signs, helpful information, or even an image of the front view displayed on the rear surface of the car.

Automation and robotics have been part of the car industry for a long time. As Industry 4.0 is accelerating, robotics, together with digitalization and artificial intelligence, is fundamentally changing industrial production; the Industry 4.0 strategy of leading car manufacturers relies on the digitalization of the entire value chain. Physical and digital processes are becoming increasingly interlaced, which lays the foundations for completely connected smart factories. With this concept, car production is also highly connected with customers, where customers' demands become guiding principles during the production of each car [64].

A smart factory is seen to be more flexible and more efficient. Greater flexibility assumes a faster response to global market changes and fluctuations as well as to customer demands. In contrast, greater efficiency means rational use of resources (e.g., energy, buildings, or material supplies). To achieve these goals, a smart factory should incorporate a completely digital process chain that exercises constant inventory control, which means that at any time and anywhere, each component in the (car) production process can be identified. Also, smart factory obtains control of production facilities from any place. Apart from flexible production processes, smart factory assumes simplified installation of new and modification of existing production facilities, which results in shorter innovation cycles, that is, product innovations can be transferred to more model series in a shorter time (time-to-market).

As all participants, that is, objects (entities) of a smart factory, are mutually connected and also connected to the Internet, the entire physical world of the production process in the smart factory can be translated into the digital world –all systems and processes are real-time mapped into digital twins [65] (even entire factory halls). In this way, the technical feasibility of any necessary operation can be estimated and clarified (i.e., précised) on the computer in advance – long before the start of mass production (of some car models). Thereby, many innovative procedures involving virtual reality and/or 3D printing may be introduced. For example, 3D printing may be used to create needed tools/objects (such as grip elements or protective covers needed in man-robot co-operation), rapid prototyping for sand-casting molds for engines, etc. Smart factories may also include machine learning in the production process. In such a case, a machine (i.e., a lightweight robot) can learn the path to be followed within the production process (when defined once) through a simple demonstration by a worker who leads the robot (as a senior worker in a factory would show all necessary steps of a given operation to a new worker) [66].

Apart from using innovative key technologies that can be incorporated into smart cars themselves or within the car production processes, Car Industry 4.0 is also oriented to the production of smart cars that possess a very important property –environment-friendly, that is, they must have zero emissions. For that reason, electric cars are becoming increasingly popular.

4.1.1 Car production chain

Car production is among the most complex production processes. Similarly, the automotive supply chain for car manufacturing is also one of the complex processes in the world. There are several challenges to face, including market globalization. Therefore, new technologies are needed to support and improve car production chains. One of the key technologies is DLT.

4.1.1.1 Supply-chain tracking

Nowadays, it is very difficult for customers to carry out true product valuations in global trade and commerce due to the non-transparency in their supply chains. Besides, it is often practically impossible to check if some goods are manufactured illegally or perhaps in an unethical way. For example, in the Democratic Republic of Congo that has about two-thirds of the world's cobalt reserves needed to produce electric cars' batteries, a significant amount of cobalt may come from mines where child labor is exploited. In such and many other situations, blockchain and other DLTs could be used to change the rules within the supply-chain of the goods toward increasing transparency and efficiency, which would certainly impact positively each phase of the supply process (warehousing, delivery, payment).

The transparency can be ensured due to the DLs' inherent property that every transaction is recorded on multiple copies over many nodes that maintain a ledger. The same is with security since the transactions are packed in blocks (in the case of blockchain), which are firmly linked and secured using cryptography. Furthermore, since a DL provides consensus and each participant in a supply chain has the same version of the ledger; disputes related to transactions are made impossible.

In a concrete example, a startup company, Circulor, has launched a project (based on blockchain technology) to track cobalt from a mine to a car battery producer [67]. An electric vehicles manufacturer that is keen to maintain its reputation as an environmentally friendly and ethical production company could use the Circulor's blockchain (i.e., its application for tracking) when deciding from which seller will it purchase cobalt (in case the company itself produces batteries) or batteries.

Similar applications could be developed for use in other sectors, for example, when the distribution of humanitarian aid (food, vaccines, money) has to be tracked to ensure that the necessary items are delivered to those who need them.

4.1.1.2 Synchronization of digital twins

Over the last few years, the growth of IoT boosted the development of several new technologies as digital twin technology [65]. In short, a digital twin is a virtual model of a process, product, or service. The model is constantly updated with the real data gathered through the connection with its physical counterpart, that is, from the various sensors embedded in the product.

One of the areas where digital twin technology increasingly finds its place is the automotive industry. For example, automotive engineers analyze the digital twin of a real car to study how the car is driven (i.e., style). They can suggest specific changes in the car with the obtained results of the analysis, which should reduce the future failure probability of the car.

To maintain a near real-time representation of a physical prototype (product), a digital twin (or digital avatar) should be continuously synchronized with the prototype. The data and values for synchronization are often exchanged over the Internet. In such a situation, using a DL such as, blockchain, tangle, or hashgraph (with its cryptographic methods) can provide secure and reliable data exchange. Thereby, the need for a central exchange instance is avoided.

4.1.1.3 Management of software versions and documents' releases

In software companies with many employees, a big challenge is tracking and managing numerous software releases, transparently and efficiently. Every change in code or update in a new release should be well documented and visible to all relevant players in the company. Distributed ledger technologies can improve the software release management cycle, including developing, testing, deploying, and supporting new software versions.

Various software-release data can be stored in a distributed ledger – the baseline documentation, development projects, changes, versioning of development, etc. The transaction logic incorporated in the distributed ledger, by design, ensures that any change of a data record initiates a new transaction/event, making the documenting process irreversible. In that way, besides achieving maximum transparency of the process, the damaging risk resulting from specific blackouts is considerably reduced.

In the second half of 2013, blockchain technology started being used for registering physical assets, giving the possibility to use the public ledger to store and validate documents instead of relying on a central authority. A user can store the signature and the timestamp associated with a document in the blockchain and validate it at any point using blockchain mechanisms. Similarly, as for software versioning, DLTs could help in tracking various documents' releases. Using a distributed ledger, a goal achieved here is that all participants can have access to documents in a secure, traceable, and transparent way, assuming that each document's release is protected against any uncoordinated change. Apart from that, a distributed ledger with a high scalability property (e.g., hashgraph or tangle) will be able to support high data volumes as well as the high frequency of documents' release.

4.1.1.4 Multi-agent robot systems

Among the numerous niches emerging from the concept of Industry 4.0 [68] where blockchains and DLTs could find their use, are multi-agent robot systems (MARSs). This term formally represents a collection of two or more autonomous mobile robots working together in a specific environment and working on different tasks. A team of mobile autonomous robots/agents working together to achieve some (well-defined) goals can be homogenous or consist of robots with different characteristics. In any case, they are allowed to communicate and coordinate with each other to be as efficient as possible (e.g., fast and with minimal consumption of energy or resources). However, finding the optimal working strategies and routines for each given objective may represent a huge challenge, even for simple tasks.

Car Industry 4.0 is highly reliant on robotics, for example, in a smart factory, several robots with different levels of autonomy and mobility should co-operate amidst dynamic and ever-changing car production processes. Therefore, the use of DLTs, as support to MARSs and generally to multi-agent systems (MASs), becomes ever more significant. In line with this, specific importance has to be given to the information support when groups of robots have to operate under external disturbances and environmental changes. Successful solutions for these could be found in the distributed ledger technology. For example, the history of interactions between robots could be recorded in a blockchain or various verification tasks could be performed using the mechanisms that have already been incorporated in the blockchain technology. In this way, the efficiency of interaction between robots (either in the car industry or generally) can be increased. The possibilities of applications that include groups of robots can be expanded.

A confirmation for this could be the appearance of several studies investigating the use of blockchain technology in MAS applications. In [68] is presented an overview and analysis of several relevant publications in this area, where the authors identified main groups of practical tasks within MARSs, which could be realized with the help of blockchain. Among studies mentioned in [68] are [69] and [70], where the interaction of the smart factory components within the company and with other industrial participants of IoT environment is investigated, providing control and trust over the distribution of products and resources. Also, there is research [71] that deals with a blockchain-based protocol that determines multi-agent control/coordination for Unmanned Aerial Vehicles (UAVs) [72].

In [73] a possible way (i.e., a methodology) of creating and operating coalitions of heterogeneous intelligent robots that use information stored in the blockchain is described. With the proposed methodology, the fast exchange of information between coalition members is assumed, and the smart contracts through which are distributed different tasks between robots, information resources, and embedded devices (e.g., tasks of control, sensory, service, or computational kind). Similarly, in [74] a modular architecture that relies on a decentralized ledger (RobotChain framework [75]) where robotic events are registered, as well as on smart contracts for sending orders to robots (robot managing) is proposed. Some of the application examples given in [74] are:
– distribution of tasks within a robot network,
– a method of assisting robots in cases when they cannot execute given tasks or need specific information, or
– voting consensus for swarm robotics.

The typical use cases of blockchain technology for MARS applications can be classified as follows [68]:

1. Distribution of commands to robots and logging robot actions and states
For example, the halls of a smart factory can be equipped with many very heterogeneous agents, such as different types of robots, intelligent devices, or computer applications/bots that can interact with each other (see Fig. 4.1). The agents, generally, do not execute predefined programs that control their behavior. Instead, they are configured to receive and execute command sequences given in some descriptive form (e.g., a bytecode). In the case of a mobile robot equipped with sensors and gripper, a batch of commands might look as follows: 1) move 20 m along the red line on the floor in a positive direction and stop; 2) rotate clockwise at the spot until detecting shelf B38; 3) approach the shelf, find the green box and bring it to device R5 in the hall C. Commands issued in a given form represent the executable code that does not depend on the platform an

agent operates on, meaning that the same executable code (i.e., bytecode) will give the same results no matter to which agent/robot it was sent (under the condition that the chosen agent is capable of executing the given commands).

Within such an arranged environment, a blockchain can be used to distribute bytecodes to robots and other agents. The agents are, thereby, not connected directly to the system which generates tasks but via a P2P network of the blockchain that maintains the nodes. Command messages to agents are saved in the blockchain. Therefore, the executing agents do not even need to be turned on at the moment of message delivery. On the other hand, the acting agent informs the network about changes of its state during the execution of the bytecode/commands (e.g., "rotated 60° clockwise", "gripped the box" or "moved backward for 10 m"), and the actual state is stored in the blockchain. In this way, if the agent halts for any reason, its state can quickly recover after the halt.

2. Optimization of task execution through economic incentives
With the blockchain's incentive mechanism, agents earn incentives (e.g., the blockchain's native tokens/cryptocurrency) when executing given tasks with minimal resources, or penalized if they behave uneconomically. These mechanisms can be used for the optimization of various production processes where robots are involved.

3. Task dispatching for maximal efficiency
The use of smart contracts based on the blockchain can create an environment with market rules. There, the task dispatching, that is, selecting agents to execute different tasks is regulated by the market, whereby, various agents/robots compete for tasks to be assigned and where the assignment of specific tasks to the appropriate agents is performed by distributed consensus, namely, a task-dispatching code stored in the blockchain (in the form of a smart contract) imposes a rollout in which a customer (or a specialized agent) first sends to the dispatcher of the smart contract, a request to perform a task, after which, the dispatcher informs the agents about the new request. Then, each of the concerned agents sends to the blockchain (via P2P network (see Fig. 4.1)) its agreement to perform the task with the information on the fee (e.g., in native tokens of the blockchain) the agent is ready to pay for handling the agreement. The blockchain validators then order the agreements received from agents according to the fees the agents offer. The first agreement, that is, the one with the highest fee offer is confirmed by the smart contract code, while the corresponding agent (the winner) receives details of the task that is to be executed.

In such a competitive environment, the agents provided with a cost optimization strategy will offer more for new tasks, to be selected by validators, as they have more money (i.e., tokens) earned from the earlier tasks, for example, through receiving rewards for the economic (i.e., optimal) behavior during the realization of these tasks (see the previous item). The overall result of such a described market competition should be that some producing process (or services) performed by a MA(R)S is stable and maximally efficient.

4. Detecting and excluding intruders or faulty agents by action validation

Apart from executing their primary tasks (defined in bytecode), at the same time, agents could be performing the validation of each other's actions, locations, or poses. For example, in a swarm (i.e., in a team of agents/robots) occupied by its general job, agents periodically send (to the blockchain P2P network) actual information from their motion sensors about their positions (and/or poses) and the positions of other agents in the swarm. With the blockchain's consensus mechanism, a consensus about the actual positions of all agents can be achieved. In this way, the hacked robots (or even the robots injected by an intruder) which misbehave intentionally could be identified, since they send pieces of information that are in conflict with the consensus.

5. Distributed decision making by a time-limited voting

Implementation of different smart contracts on the blockchain can enable a complex behavior of a MARS-like time-limited voting or voting delegation, namely, certain concrete actions (formulated in bytecode) can be proposed by a group of smart-contract agents, while another group of agents can vote for actions. The result is an action scenario gathered through the collaboration of multiple agents, which can then be stored in the blockchain and distributed to the concerned agents/robots (see Fig. 4.1), and finally executed.

6. Authentication/suitability check

Complex MARS systems tend to be as efficient as possible. There might arise situations when some agents/robots use a shared physical resource but do not trust each other (as they may possess a certain level of artificial intelligence), which may cause undesirable consequences. Such situations may be resolved through appropriate decentralized applications based on blockchain, which involves methods for agents' authentication or checking agents' suitability. The mistrust among robots is erased, and possible conflicts are avoided.

4.1.2 Car features and use

Novel and innovative technologies are at the core of the automotive industry, enabling the launch of new car features and their continuous improvement, aiming for user-friendly and popular services for car owners and drivers. Distributed ledger technology offers various possibilities for incorporating several car features in the present and future automotive systems, including autonomous driving.

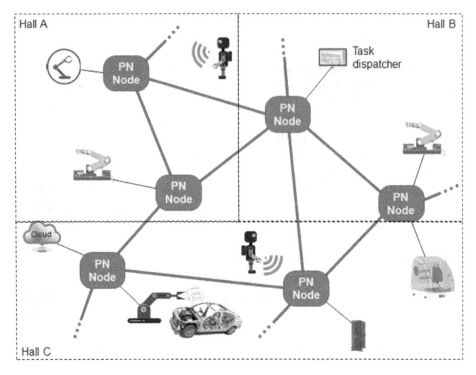

Fig. 4.1: Blockchain P2P network supporting a MARS in a car producing smart factory (an illustration).

4.1.2.1 Autonomous driving systems

Leading carmakers and numerous start-ups are investing in a lot of research related to the DLT's possible use to enhance autonomous driving systems, that is, in overcoming various problems that self-driving cars may encounter. Autonomous driving systems are significantly functional, for now. Self-driving cars can currently collect and process huge amounts of data from their environment every second so that they can successfully avoid barriers, find optimal paths in curves, optimize speed by the control of acceleration and braking, etc. However, the hardware used cannot support complex computations needed to drive an autonomous car safely through an intersection. Adding more cars into the equation increases the amount and the complexity of computations exponentially.

At the moment, however, the problem is that, when entering an intersection, a self-driving car cannot know and predict the behavior of the nearby cars (especially the ones coming from the front). So, as vehicles cannot trust each other, all autonomous cars must be prepared for the worst case at the intersection. The solution, which could bypass the problem, is the presence of a road-master – a central entity which decides what happens on the road and at what moment. Each car entering the intersection sends its current and desired location to the road-master, while the road-master calculates the next step of each car and orders some cars to move and others to wait. Even then, the problem of mistrust persists, since in some cases, cars might not obey the instructions (e.g., when a car is in a hurry due to an urgent situation or when the system is hacked). This is where blockchain (or some other DL) technology may be applied and help remove some of the trust issues.

To be more specific, the blockchain-driven autonomous cars will trust each other, while a blockchain-based DApp will calculate the flow of cars in a decentralized manner. In such a system, cars will still be instructed to wait, when needed, but the wait times will be fairly distributed among the vehicles. Since each car will be assured that no other car will ever cross its path, self-driven cars will not be paranoid . They will not have to analyze situations and act assuming the worst-case scenario every time they pass an intersection. Apart from that, due to security mechanisms incorporated in blockchain technology, hacker attacks would be impossible. Privacy concerns are also overcome, since blockchains can provide anonymity as well.

There is a way of DLT improving the autonomous driving systems; it is through data recording and sharing. Each self-driving car might collect data about the trip and save it in a DL. The data may contain various useful information, for example, local traffic density, weather conditions, warnings about accidents, traffic patterns, etc. As a result, these data can be accessed by other cars in the network.

4.1.2.2 Secure lock/unlock of vehicles

There is another future characteristic of the cars for the humans –the owners of the future cars that are blockchain technology incorporated will be able to lock and unlock their cars via smartphones in a much more secure and faster way (i.e., less than 2 s). This will be possible thanks to a direct offline connection between the owner's smartphone application and the car, that is, without the involvement of any third-party central server, as is now the case with most of the conventional methods. The weak point of these methods is that the vehicle could be unlocked, without permission, if the server is hacked. With a decentralized and secure blockchain, all of this is avoided. Thereby, the security of the unlocking process is improved due to cryptographic encryption of the established connection.

Additionally, since all log data in the blockchain are written without the possibility of being changed, the owner will be able to track all car activities through the application. Besides, the owner could grant temporary access to the car to some other person (e.g., to a friend if he/she forgot something in the car), even if the owner is far away from the car. This can be done by transferring the access rights onto another person over a remote transaction. To get access to the car from its owner, the third party does not need additional hardware. The transfer of the access rights is achieved by simply using a smart contract, which triggers the transaction if, say, the car owner gives a command via their smartphone app. At the same time, the owner receives real-time notifications about who accessed the car, and where and when.

4.1.2.3 Car-related payments

With regard to payments concerning vehicles concerning, it is now known that DLT can be used for different types of payments. For example, upon charging the battery of an electric car, a smart contract based on the Ethereum blockchain (or maybe on the hashgraph) could trigger a transaction to pay for the service of charging, whereby, the money is transferred from the account of the car owner to the account of the charging station.

Another possibility is a financial application (or an extension of it) for payment, in instalments, of the car itself. In this case, a smart contract would trigger a transaction on the first of each month, which transfers the appropriate instalment amount from the buyer's account to the car selling company's account. The cumulative balance would also be recorded in the blockchain; so, the smart contract would stop payments once the balance reaches the car's price. The same financial application could be used for other car-related services, for example, periodic payments of insurance, monthly payments for parking, etc., but also for many other payments not necessarily related to cars.

4.1.2.4 Protection of mileage reading against tampering

The most manipulated parameter related to cars so far is the car's mileage displayed on the car's front panel. In the future, the risk of mileage tampering would be practically zero if the current mileage of a vehicle is written regularly (i.e., periodically or after each ride) in a DL, such as tangle, hashgraph, or blockchain. Together with the mileage, many other parameters including the data about the actual position of the vehicle (GPS coordinates) could be written in the distributed ledger. In this way, the use of DLTs would enable not only an absolutely secure information about the total mileage, but also provide a reliable tracking of the vehicle's journey of the past, starting from the very moment it was delivered from the factory.

4.1.2.5 Serial numbers handling – registering and management

Instead of keeping records about pure transactions of some cryptocurrency, a blockchain or any other type of DL structure can also be used to securely keep various data, for example, serial numbers of various products or digests/digital signatures of some important documents, etc.

In this way, a distributed ledger, in which serial numbers of vehicles' parts or serial numbers of some expensive products' components are written, represents a powerful framework that cannot be counterfeited. This counterfeiting became a big problem, especially in the luxury goods industry. Each piece of a product (e.g., a part of the car engine, a watch, a gemstone, etc.) with a serial number affixed directly on it in the production stage by a manufacturer can be protected against forgery. Its authenticity is easily confirmed if the serial number is, at the same time, written into a DL. The information written in the distributed ledger can also contain the manufacturing date, its producer or assembler, the history of repairs (if any), the owner (after purchasing), etc.

Allocating and assigning serial numbers to the components, adding other relevant data, and generating corresponding records to be written in the distributed ledger could be carried via an appropriate application that connects to the DL, product manufacturer, and customers. The use of such a DL-based application would eliminate the need for physical certificates, such as warranty cards or product data sheets, which so far represent the global standard for proving the authenticity of (luxury) products. Without these certificates, which can be forged, the sale of counterfeit goods is practically erased.

4.1.2.6 Digital proof of ownership by the use of registers

It is not just serial numbers and the data related to products that are seen as content (different from transactions) that can be written in DLs. Another example is the data related to all types of property – land titles, software license numbers, vehicle identification numbers (VINs), etc. DLs can serve as registries to confirm any product or property ownership rights. A transaction is created concerning the physical asset to register the ownership of an asset. Moreover, the information is stored in a blockchain record, and the owner of the private key is then registered as the owner of that asset.

Furthermore, with the use of blockchains, for example, the transfer of ownership from an original owner (who has sold some asset or property) to a new owner can be automatically done through a simple, safe, and secure operation on the blockchain, that is, by the execution of a smart contract on that blockchain.

4.2 Smart mobility

The development of smart cities, villages [76], and Smart Energy solutions are also included in the development of smart mobility. As one of the most important global industries, the mobility industry faces the biggest and deepest change in its history, caused by climate change, urbanization, and social developments, thus leading to changed and continuously changing customer requirements. Novel technologies, like DLT, enable an easier integration of smart solutions into the car and mobility industries.

4.2.1 Inspiring car driving in an environmentally responsible way

Cryptocurrencies, that is, tokens for special purposes, can be achieved by DLT as well. Such a token system would motivate participants to behave in a certain positive way, which may eventually be turned into positive habits of some participants.

The arrangement should motivate drivers to operate their cars in a responsible and eco-friendly manner. As a reward, a driver who joined the project receives a certain amount of coins, whenever he/she, in some specific traffic situations, follows some recommended rules for responsible driving, for example, when the engine is switched to ECO mode, when driving is as smooth as possible (without sudden braking and acceleration), when driver coasts to stop, etc.

The driving data from a vehicle is sent to an application that processes it and calculates the height of the driver reward. At the same time, each transaction to the driver's account is written in the blockchain.

4.2.2 Parking reservation

All drivers are quite aware that finding a parking place in a big city is often quite an issue. The solution, which can make it easier, could rely on DLT. When a vehicle leaves the place where it was parked temporarily, a relevant piece of information can be sent to a corresponding data marketplace. Through a DLT-based application, other drivers in the vicinity can receive that information and, if necessary, generate a transaction to reserve the released parking place. The application could also provide additional help to the driver, for example, propose the best parking place (if there are several unreserved places), depending on actual traffic conditions and the driver's position on the road, navigate the vehicle to the chosen parking place, etc.

4.2.3 Car and ride sharing

The use of distributed ledger technologies, t, applications regarding payments in cryptocurrencies, is also a current precondition of various services. The applications may or may not be based on smart contracts.

One of the ideas anticipated to be realized soon is autonomous car renting. The service would be similar to today's ride-hailing services (e.g., Uber), except that cars will not have drivers, and the payments will be in a cryptocurrency, such as IOTA or Bitcoin. Additionally, a car owner would be given the opportunity of earning by placing his car at the disposal of others whenever the owner does not use it.

Apart from that, a future DL-based application might enable ride sharing and the sharing of car ownership, where a group of people would share a fleet of several autonomous vehicles. When a member of the group needs a ride, he or she will request access to a car, available at that moment, via an application. In the respective DL, all activities of the cars in the fleet would be recorded. As regards the maintenance costs of the entire fleet, they could be regulated through a payment model that is agreed upon among the owners. For example, paying a fee (into a shared account) every time an owner uses a car, according to the total distance traveled, or monthly payments according to the frequency of cars' use of an owner compared to the total use of cars from the fleet by all owners, etc.

4.2.4 Traffic congestion management

Similarly, various information can be shared and written in a distributed ledger, in cases of traffic obstructions (due to accidents, wildfires, floods, landslides, etc.). The relevant information, collected and compared by the participants familiar with obstructions on their ways, can be acquired by other approaching vehicles in the vicinity, to change their routes on time and avoid possible holdup and consequent delay.

4.3 Smart energy

A traditional electric grid is an interconnected system for the production, transmission, and delivery of electricity. The grid dynamically balances the demand and supply of electric energy to assure stability and reliability of grid operation. Its immense economic dimension is reflected in the need for accurate measurements of consumption, and well-defined billing and trading mechanisms among actors involved in the electricity demand and supply. The electric grid is one of the critical infrastructures and is thus essential for almost any economic and social activity in the world.

A smart grid (SG) opens traditional electric grids, in terms of communication and interoperability, and leverages new operational and business models related to electrical energy production, transport, storage, and consumption. In terms of deployment, smart grids can be considered an example of a highly geo-distributed IoT system with high security and trust requirements. New technological developments and new business, economic, and environmental expectations lead to a gradual transformation toward a smart grid concept. A smart grid is heavily based on information and communication technologies, applied to the electricity domain. It enables new and innovative use cases in the utilities domain, which are technically infeasible in the traditional electric grid.

The latest trends in this area are called Smart Energy, Internet of Energy, or Energy Internet (EI). They indicate the ambition of sharing both energy and the related data just as we are used to sharing information on the Internet. This means that, for example, participants can interact closely, make autonomous decisions, seamlessly access different distributed and centralized energy resources, share energy to balance energy demand and supply, and act as prosumers – producers or consumers of electrical power, or both. Blockchain technologies can efficiently support these novel developments and ambitions for allowing data and monetary transactions for energy trading. Applying distributed ledger is a viable option to provide a secure, transparent, trusted, automated workflow for the advanced future Energy Internet services. However, the practical application of DLTs in a smart grid infrastructure is far from being straightforward.

4.3.1 Smart grid conceptual model

The electric grid is a hierarchically structured system. The structure results from the geographical disposition of the grid segments and affects the roles of the actors involved in the grid operation. A systematic smart grid architectural model [77] helps achieve interoperability across technical domains and different stakeholders of the massively scaled, distributed SG system. A service-oriented approach was taken regarding cross-business impacts. The model provides the stakeholders a common understanding of the elements that make up the smart grid and provides guidance for the implementation architecture. In the smart grid conceptual model, which is a part of the architectural model, NIST divided the smart grid into seven domains, as shown in Fig. 4.2. Each domain encompasses smart grid conceptual roles and services.

The customer domain refers to the end-users of electricity, who may also generate, store, and manage energy use. Usually, three customer types are discussed, each with its sub-domain: home, commercial/building, and industrial. In the markets domain, there are the operators and participants in electricity markets, and in the service provider domain, the organizations provide services to electrical customers and utilities. The operations refer to managers of the movement of electricity. In the generation domain are the generators of electricity, including traditional generation sources and distributed energy resources. In the transmission domain are the carriers of bulk electricity over long distances, and in the distribution domain are the distributors of electricity to and from customers. Generation, transmission and distribution domains may also store electricity.

The three customer sub-domains –the home, the commercial/building, and the industrial, differ in energy needs and distribution scale. Actors in the customer domain provide customers with the electrical flows. Apart from that, they provide the information flow between the customer domain and other domains. The boundaries of the customer domain are usually the utility meter or the home gateway (also referred to as the energy service interface, ESI). The gateway securely interconnects the outbound and the inbound communications; it may communicate with other domains via the advanced metering infrastructure (AMI) or the Internet. It faces the facility-based systems, such as a home or building automation system. The customer domain directly interacts with the distribution, operations, markets, and service provider domains.

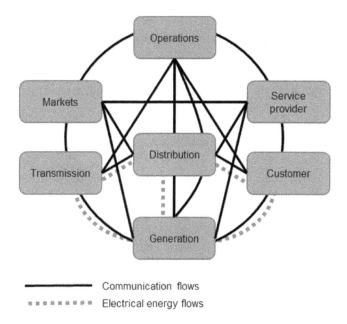

—————— Communication flows

▪▪▪▪▪▪▪▪▪ Electrical energy flows

Fig. 4.2: Interaction of roles in different smart grid domains: energy and communication flows.

4.3.2 Decentralization in the energy internet

A challenge in meeting the requirements of modern smart grid applications is the inclusion of decentralized technologies in SG architectures, and the related use and business scenarios. Current and future use cases could include:
- Distributed energy resource (DER) management and peer-to-peer energy trading;
- Autonomous islands of energy prosumers, where supply and demand for energy are first cleared within the island, and the excess is bought/sold to the grid; microgrids;
- Multi-tenancy, innovative payment models for energy in retail and wholesale markets, which combine payments in excessive energy, utility tokens, crypto-currencies, etc.;
- Electric vehicle charging and coordination;
- Blockchain-enabled prepaid electricity meters;
- Automated machine-to-machine negotiation for bidding the terms and placing the order for energy to the most convenient provider;
- Providing open data from the smart grid to facilitate third-party application and service development;
- Green and environmental aspects of energy production and consumption.

A valuable, yet straightforward, application of the DLT can be recording data and events from the smart grid. This might include consumption and generation-related information (smart meters with BC support) or data about the operation of the smart grid (management information, key performance indicator reports, aggregated usage values, etc.).

But, let's consider a more advanced smart grid use case of a family residing in a small private house. The family commutes daily using a plug-in electric vehicles (PEV), which is recharged at home or work. The household is an active prosumer, trying to be as self-independent in energy supply as possible. It has, therefore, photovoltaic panels installed on the roof of the house. A power bank installed in the house's basement can store some of the excess electricity produced, for later use. The remaining unused electricity can be traded automatically with some of the neighbors. Therefore, the neighborhood is subscribed to an automated aggregation service, which optimizes neighborhood electricity demand and supply and acts as one larger actor to external energy providers. If home and neighborhood production does not meet the current demand, electricity is negotiated for in the market. All these procedures are executed automatically and exchange of electricity is simultaneously paid with micropayments, which are transparently logged. The family can, therefore, always verify that the system works for their best benefit. The latter is true for all the other actors involved in this use case, too.

A home automation system and energy management system balances the energy from the in-house energy resources with the demand and in-house storage. The home automation system estimates the acceptable range of the required electricity in a household for a certain future period. It considers the settings made by the user (desired level of comfort in the house), the known daily schedule of the family members, and the weather forecast. It can reschedule some larger loads, such as charging a PEV, heating water, drying the clothes, etc. A distributed ledger is not required in this segment if the customer privately owns the home automation and the energy management system. A home gateway needs to link both in-house systems with a DL network for trusted interaction with other actors.

If the demand and supply in the household are imbalanced, the excess energy can be bought or sold to the neighbors in the local district, namely, an organized cooperative which balances the demand and the distributed resources installed in the several households in the neighborhood. The exchange of electricity among the neighbors is recorded in a smart contract and cleared with the corresponding exchange for utility tokens. These can later be sold or reused to purchase electricity.

In this way, the microgrid aggregates the individual households into a new, larger prosuming actor. The aggregation is backed by a smart contract, too, and is entirely automated. There is no need for an aggregation service provider in terms of a legal or business entity. This reduces the operating costs of aggregation. Besides, scaling up the demand and supply enables them to participate more autonomously in the energy market. Aggregation into a larger entity offers them a better price negotiation position with the external electricity providers. The aggregating system can automatically negotiate with several power providers for the best electricity price. Smart contracts make the bidding and selection, and the result is verifiable by every involved party.

Similarly, the microgrid can act as a tertiary reserve for temporary deficits of energy production elsewhere. In that case, the microgrid aggregator would receive an offer (in the form of a DL transaction) from the distribution or transport smart grid domains. It would then issue requests to acquire some of the energy from PEVs or local storage in the individual homes. The charging stations at customers' homes would estimate the amount of energy at their disposal based on the car battery status and foreseen travel plans derived from customers' online calendars, and bid for sale. When the tertiary reserves are activated, the power provided in the emergency case has substantially higher prices than the regular. The benefits would be shared among the household involved, according to the rules in the smart contract.

Several aspects of the use cases described here have been implemented and tested at a smaller level. The benefits and optimizations might seem small, if observed from a single customer's perspective. However, the application of DLs enables scaling of such approaches, seamless operation due to smart contract automation, and reduction of operating expenses by the elimination of intermediaries.

4.3.2.1 Requirements for distributed ledger technologies

Several distinguishing aspects of smart grids affect the role and adoption of distributed ledger technology for the decentralized Energy Internet. Despite the successful introduction of ICT in the SG, grid systems remain relatively closed and centralized with regard to ownership and governance. However, this concept is gradually changing. Nevertheless, (smart) grid remains a critical infrastructure. It is mostly regulated and is characterized by an immense business perspective and possible financial implications. At the same time, it presents a highly distributed and heterogeneous system, especially in the customer domain. It is characterized by a large and dispersed customer base and by the various technologies for the communication connectivity needed for the communication flows of smart grid applications. Incessant connectivity of customer devices, for example, smart meters, cannot always be assumed. A blockchain architecture for the smart grid must, therefore, be able to balance between the availability and consistency of data in case network partitions are caused, for example, due to a temporary loss of communication connectivity. Such an architecture can, further, be hierarchical to match the hierarchical structure of the grid itself. The hierarchical structure of the blockchain data is also beneficial to limit the scope of data generated in various segments of the smart grid, for performance and privacy. Therefore, the DL networks for the Energy Internet are often implemented as hybrid blockchain networks or specialized public/consortium networks.

The financial aspects of decentralized Energy Internet applications are commonly addressed by tokenization. Many decentralized Energy Internet platforms (see examples in Section 4.3.3) introduce their tokens for energy trading, certificate exchange, or loyalty and incentive programs. There are decentralized platform providers that are specialized in Energy Internet. Their products are reaching a level of maturity required for a broader and large-scale adoption of decentralized solutions. Often, lack of regulations is a more limiting factor for adoption than technology.

4.3.2.2 Energy web decentralized ecosystem for energy internet

Energy Web Foundation[61] provides the Energy Web Decentralized Operating System[62] (EW-DOS). It is an enterprise-grade open-source stack of decentralized software and standards, middleware services, and software development toolkits (SDK), including the EW Chain. EW Chain is a purpose-built public blockchain network designed for the energy sector's regulatory, operational, and market needs.

The chain was designed to overcome some of the cost, scalability, and power consumption problems facing traditional public blockchains, when used for energy sector applications. It is a Proof of Authority consortium network with validator nodes hosted by tens of companies. Known corporations run validator nodes within the affiliate ecosystem, including some of the largest and most respected energy companies globally. EW Chain addresses user privacy. The mechanism of private transactions is a way of encrypting certain energy transaction details to comply with personal data regulations. Light clients enable the integration of IoT devices. Apart from the blockchain network, the EW-DOS delivers several suits of SDKs for integration and application development. The EW Flex enables grid operators to integrate distributed energy resources (DERs) into energy markets and demand flexibility in programs. The EW Origin supports existing and emerging renewable energy and carbon markets to simplify and enhance the issuance, tracking, and buying/selling of energy attribute certificates.

EW Chain and EW DOS managed to generate substantial interest in the decentralized Energy Internet communities, and several relevant projects utilize parts of this ecosystem. The main use cases are clean energy and carbon emissions traceability, distributed energy resource flexibility for distribution (DSO) and transmission system operators (TSO), and electric vehicle charging. Running their DApp on EW Chain should allow the operators to reduce transaction costs and scale up demand response programs, more quickly and efficiently.

4.3.3 Smart energy use cases

Decentralization in the Energy Internet is an active field of research prototyping and development, and demonstrating practical projects, trials, and commercial implementations, which have been successfully running for several years. The most prominent

---

61 https://www.energyweb.org
62 https://www.energyweb.org/technology/ew-dos/

area is a peer-to-peer energy trading, combined with distributed energy resource management and green energy. The other focus is more on decentralization in retail and wholesale trading. Energy supply and origin certificates are commonly tokenized with distributed ledger technology to facilitate novel and flexible trading mechanisms with tradable tokens.

4.3.3.1 Distributed energy resources and peer-to-peer energy trading

Small energy resources, for example, solar or wind plants, boost the environment and reduce electricity costs. Unlike the traditional central power plants, they are highly distributed. Renewable energy resources depend on unpredictable factors such as the weather and are, therefore, heavily volatile in energy production. DERs usually belong to different proprietors. To be more efficient, they can be aggregated in microgrids. Microgrids are clusters of jointly managed DERs located in proximity. They can be organized as a cooperative, which balances the demand and the supplies of the distributed resources installed in several households in a district, and trades the excessive energy production. Peer-to-peer energy trading is one of the keys to such a balance. Even if a microgrid is not fully self-sustainable, P2P trading reduces the dependence on central power resources and reduces electricity costs.

Blockchain technologies have successfully integrated into microgrid aggregation, distributed resources and storage, and P2P energy trading. It is estimated that more than half of the distributed DL energy Internet projects are about peer-to-peer energy markets. This makes P2P trading, the dominant use case for DLT in the Energy Internet.

The Suncontract[63] is a decentralized marketplace for households and businesses. It has successfully been in operation for several years. It minimizes the costs for energy customers. It uses a globally recognized, tradeable token (the SNC token) to buy and sell energy products on the SunContract ecosystem.

LO3 Energy[64] is a DLT platform provider for the Energy Internet. Their Pando platform offers a simple way to account for the local distributed energy and enable new incentives for customers. LO3 Energy is the founder and technology provider for Brooklyn Microgrid, BMG.[65] BMG is a marketplace that allows prosumers, that is, residential and commercial solar panel owners, to sell the excess solar energy they generate to NYC residents, who prefer using renewable energy over fossil fuel energy.

Power Ledger[66] is another platform for new energy markets to track and trade energy, flexible services, and environmental commodities.

---

63 https://suncontract.org/
64 https://lo3energy.com/
65 https://www.brooklyn.energy/
66 https://www.powerledger.io/

4.3.3.2 Retail and wholesale electricity marketplaces

In retail and wholesale electricity trading, high-quality data, near real-time operation, continuous bidding and instant settlements, transparent contracts, minimizing counterparty risks, including partner credit evaluations and payments, are requirements that are successfully met by DLT.

The Drift Trader[67] facilitates build a FinTech platform and a marketplace to help companies match their energy purchases with local clean energy supply, in real-time. Power Purchase Agreements are virtualized and converted to smart contracts. In this way, corporations can access the benefits of high-frequency trading with other algorithmic trading platform participants.

With the WePower[68] platform, companies of all sizes can easily buy green energy directly from producers. They provide services for wholesale and P2P trading and assure complete (green) energy source transparency.

The system adopted a blockchain token – WPR. It stores tangible values and ensures liquidity. It constantly accrues energy donated by energy producers and accumulates real value in the form of energy.

4.3.3.3 Green and environmental energy aspects

Certification of energy origin has become extremely important. Compliance and voluntary green credits, and carbon credits markets have started emerging. These credits are tradable, non-tangible energy commodities, which prove the exact origin of energy, helping demonstrate the provenance of renewable energy supplies, or that the consumption matches the actual production in a green plant. However, these energy attribute certificate (EAC) markets are frequently fragmented and lack a value for cross-market exchange. But, global markets are needed here, including renewable energy certificates (REC), guarantees of origin (GO), and international I-REC, especially CO_2 certificates. Blockchain offers to track energy production in a much more granular and timely way than is possible by traditional methods. Some of the existing decentralized energy trading platforms (see Section 4.3.3.1) now support green credits and certificates. Power Ledger, for example, added the blockchain-based trades of renewable energy certificates in the U.S. At the same time, several successful dedicated platforms for tradable renewable certificates have emerged and have been successfully deployed.

FlexiDAO[69] is a software provider created to accelerate the transition toward a decarbonized and decentralized energy industry, leveraging blockchain applications. It offers white-label blockchain applications on top of a middleware platform that can access any blockchain infrastructure in an enterprise-grade, secure manner. FlexiDAO

---

67 https://www.drifttrader.com/
68 https://wepower.com
69 https://www.flexidao.com/

tracks the production of renewable energy from its origin in real-time and prevents double-counting.

Energy Origin[70] is a web platform built on top of low-energy Blockchain technology. It records the generation and consumption of green energy, calculates the volumes of energy exchanged between the renewable assets and customers' sites, the impact of avoided CO_2, and registers this information in tamper-proof certificates for transparency.

The Greeneum[71] platform offers several decentralized applications for the energy sector, including green certificates and carbon credits for green energy producers. The certificate determines the energy source, amount, and corresponding carbon credits. For energy trading, consumers can sell carbon credits in the marketplace.

The Universal Protocol (UP) Alliance created the world's first tradable carbon token on a public blockchain – UPCO2.[72] The UPCO2 tokens represent a certified measure of carbon dioxide. They can be bought and held as an investment or burned to offset a company's or an individual's carbon footprint. Underlying certified REDD + carbon credits back the token, and blockchain technology is a way to prevent double counting (or double-spending) of carbon credits.

4.3.3.4 Energy metering, billing, and network data management

A prerequisite for most Energy Internet applications is the integration of smart meters and blockchain platforms. Smart consumption meters are a part of the advanced metering infrastructure, which is readily deployed in modern energy grids. AMI measures, collects, and analyzes energy usage. A smart meter has a two-way communication channel, usually assured by power-line communications (PLC), or mobile (e.g., LTE/5 G), or low-power mobile (e.g., NB-IoT), or long-range WAN networks (e.g., LoRaWAN). Apart from consumption recording, AMI may support demand-side optimization or outage management too. Smart meters usually do not have unique digital decentralized identifiers and are simple transaction issuers (see Section 3.5.2). Instead, all blockchain functions are provided by AMI gateways or even by the backend blockchain platforms. This enables reuse of the installed metering infrastructure, but BC identification at the level of individual meters could yield a far more accurate, verifiable, and efficient process. An early demonstration was Bankymoon's prepaid smart meter. It was a Bitcoin-based billing system for smart meters that operated in partnership with the crowdfunding platform, Usizo. Donors could transfer cryptocurrency to third-world schools equipped with a smart meter to provide energy directly to the school of their choice.

---

70 https://theenergyorigin.com/
71 https://www.greeneum.net/
72 https://uphold.com/en/assets/environmental/buy-upco2

Swether is a prototype of an end-to-end solution based on an Ethereum BC-controlled IoT electric switch and meter [78]. This DApp comprises of the hardware and software for the IoT device, smart contract, and Ethereum-compliant Web applications for the use and control of the system. The Swether device can be built into, for example, an electric car charging station and acts as an independent BC entity, reporting the measurement status to the chain. The smart contract in the DApp tracks the availability of charging stations, enables booking a charging station for a selected period, and handles the charging payments. The smart contract allows additional payment and workflow features, such as escrow (to increase the security of involved stakeholders), bidding (to select automatically among the different available energy providers), and a system of loyalty tokens for the clients (additional incentives for service use).

References

[1]   S. Nakamoto, 'Bitcoin: A Peer-to-Peer Electronic Cash System', 2008. [Online]. Available: https://bitcoin.org/en/bitcoin-paper

[2]   S. Popov, 'The Tangle', IOTA, v1.4.3, Apr. 2018. [Online]. Available: https://assets.ctfassets. net/r1dr6vzfxhev/2t4uxvslqk0EUau6g2sw0g/45eae33637ca92f85dd9f4a3a218e1ec/ iota1_4_3.pdf

[3]   D. L. Baird, M. Harmon, and P. Madsen, 'Hedera: A Public Hashgraph Network & Governing Council', V.2.1, Aug. 2020. [Online]. Available: https://hedera.com/hh_whitepaper_v2.1-20200815.pdf

[4]   E. Lombrozo, J. Lau, and P. Wuille, 'Segregated Witness (Consensus layer)', Bitcoin, Bitcoin BIP, Dec. 2015. (Accessed Jun. 04, 2021). [Online]. Available: https://github.com/bitcoin/ bips/blob/master/bip-0141.mediawiki

[5]   R. C. Merkle, 'A digital signature based on a conventional encryption function', in *Advances in Cryptology – CRYPTO '87*, Berlin, Heidelberg, 1988, vol. LNCS, volume 293, 369–378, doi:10.1007/3-540-48184-2_32.

[6]   L. Lamport, R. Shostak, and M. Pease, 'The Byzantine Generals Problem', *ACM Transactions on Programming Languages and Systems*, 4, 3, 382–401, Jul 1982,doi:10.1145/357172. 357176.

[7]   P. Feldman and S. Micali, 'An Optimal Probabilistic Protocol for Synchronous Byzantine Agreement', *SIAM Journal on Computing*, 26, 4, 873–933, Aug 1997, doi: 10.1137/ S0097539790187084.

[8]   Mark, '51% Attack Explained', *Mycryptopedia*, Jan. 08, 2019. https://www.mycryptopedia. com/51-percent-attack-explained/ (Accessed Jun. 04, 2021).

[9]   S. Driscoll, 'How Bitcoin Works Under the Hood', *Scott Driscoll's Blog*, Jul. 14, 2013. http://www.imponderablethings.com/2013/07/how-bitcoin-works-under-hood.html (Accessed Jun. 04, 2021).

[10] M. Apostolaki, A. Zohar, and L. Vanbever, 'Hijacking Bitcoin: Routing Attacks on Cryptocurrencies', in *2017 IEEE Symposium on Security and Privacy (SP)*, San Jose, CA, May 2017, 375–392. doi: 10.1109/SP.2017.29.

[11] B. Kaiser, M. Jurado, and A. Ledger, 'The Looming Threat of China: An Analysis of Chinese Influence on Bitcoin', *arXiv:1810.02466 [cs]*, Oct. 2018, Accessed Jun. 04, 2021. [Online]. Available: http://arxiv.org/abs/1810.02466

[12] J. R. Douceur, 'The sybil attack', in *Peer-to-Peer Systems*, Berlin, Heidelberg, 2002, vol. LNCS, volume Vol. 2429, 251–260, doi: 10.1007/3-540-45748-8_24.

[13] W. Penard and T. Van Werkhoven, 'On the Secure Hash Algorithm Family', *Cryptography in context*, 1–18, 2008.

[14] 'IOTA Fundation'. https://www.iota.org (Accessed Jun. 04, 2021).

[15] 'IOTA: A Distributed Ledger of Everything for the Emerging Machine Economy', *CryptoBrowser*, Nov. 15, 2018. https://cryptobrowser.io/news/iota-a-distributed-ledger-of-everything-for-the-emerging-machine-economy (Accessed Jun. 04, 2021).

[16] K. Wu, Y. Ma, G. Huang, and X. Liu, 'A First Look at Blockchain-Based Decentralized Applications', *Software: Practice & Experience*, n/a, spe.2751, 1–18, Oct 2019, doi: 10.1002/ spe.2751.

[17] 'Clients – ethernodes.org – The Ethereum Network & Node Explorer'. https://ethernodes.org/ ?synced=1 (Accessed May 06, 2020).

[18] 'Ethereum Node Tracker | Etherscan'. https://etherscan.io/nodetracker# (Accessed May 06, 2020).

[19] 'Global Bitcoin nodes distribution'. https://bitnodes.io/ (Accessed Aug. 13, 2020).

https://doi.org/10.1515/9783110681130-005

[20] J. Ruiz, 'Public-Permissioned blockchains as Common-Pool Resources | LinkedIn', Feb. 13, 2020. https://www.linkedin.com/pulse/public-permissioned-blockchains-common-pool-resources-jesus-ruiz/ (Accessed Aug. 18, 2020).

[21] Q. Feng, D. He, S. Zeadally, M. K. Khan, and N. Kumar, 'A Survey on Privacy Protection in Blockchain System', *Journal of Network and Computer Applications*, 126, 45–58, Jan. 2019, doi: 10.1016/j.jnca.2018.10.020.

[22] 'Blockchain performance issues and limitations | Hacker Noon'. https://hackernoon.com/blockchain-performance-issues-and-limitations-78qss3co5 (Accessed Aug. 20, 2020).

[23] 'Hyperledger Blockchain Performance Metrics White Paper (1.0.1)', The Hyperledger Performance and Scale Working Gro, Whitepaper, Oct. 2018. Accessed Aug. 20, 2020. [Online]. Available: https://www.hyperledger.org/resources/publications/blockchain-performance-metrics

[24] 'The Key Metrics to Measure Blockchain Network Performance | Hacker Noon'. https://hackernoon.com/how-to-measure-blockchain-network-performance-key-metrics-en1234u4 (Accessed Aug. 20, 2020).

[25] M. Pustišek, A. Umek, and A. Kos, 'Approaching the Communication Constraints of Ethereum-Based Decentralized Applications', *Sensors*, 19, 11, 2647, Jan. 2019, doi: 10.3390/s19112647.

[26] P. Zheng, Z. Zheng, X. Luo, X. Chen, and X. Liu, 'A Detailed and Real-Time Performance Monitoring Framework for Blockchain Systems', in *2018 IEEE/ACM 40th International Conference on Software Engineering: Software Engineering in Practice Track (ICSE-SEIP)*, May 2018, 134–143.

[27] N. Szabo, 'Smart Contracts: Building Blocks for Digital Markets', *Extropy: Journal of Transhumanist Thought*, vol. 16, 1996, Accessed Aug. 10, 2020. [Online]. Available: https://www.fon.hum.uva.nl/rob/Courses/InformationInSpeech/CDROM/Literature/LOTwinterschool2006/szabo.best.vwh.net/smart_contracts_2.html

[28] N. Gopie, 'What are Smart Contracts on Blockchain?', *Blockchain Pulse: IBM Blockchain Blog*, Jul. 02, 2018. https://www.ibm.com/blogs/blockchain/2018/07/what-are-smart-contracts-on-blockchain/ (Accessed Apr. 02, 2020).

[29] A. M. Antonopoulos and G. Wood, *Mastering Ethereum – Building Smart Contracts and DApps*. O'Reilly Media, 2018. Accessed Apr. 02, 2020. [Online]. Available: http://shop.oreilly.com/product/0636920056072.do

[30] C. Cachin, 'Architecture of the Hyperledger Blockchain Fabric', presented at the ACM Symposium on Principles of Distributed Computing, Chicago, Illinois, USA, Jul. 2016. Accessed Apr. 28, 2020. [Online]. Available: https://www.zurich.ibm.com/dccl/#program

[31] 'What is an ABI and Why is it Needed to Interact with Contracts?', *Ethereum Stack Exchange*. https://ethereum.stackexchange.com/questions/234/what-is-an-abi-and-why-is-it-needed-to-interact-with-contracts (Accessed Jun. 05, 2020).

[32] 'Hyperledger Architecture, Volume II – Smart Contracts', Linux Foundation Networking, White paper, Apr. 2018. [Online]. Available: https://www.hyperledger.org/wp-content/uploads/2018/04/Hyperledger_Arch_WG_Paper_2_SmartContracts.pdf

[33] 'How does Hyperledger Fabric's Execute-order-validate Architecture work?', *Stack Overflow*. https://stackoverflow.com/questions/53136193/how-does-hyperledger-fabrics-exercute-order-validate-architecture-work (Accessed Jun. 15, 2021).

[34] Leonardo, *leonardoalt/ethereum_formal_verification_overview*. 2020. Accessed May 31, 2020. [Online]. Available: https://github.com/leonardoalt/ethereum_formal_verification_overview

[35] 'MythX Smart Contract Weakness Classification (SWC) coverage and status'. https://mythx.io/detectors/ (Accessed Jun. 15, 2020).

[36] *melonproject/oyente*. melonproject, 2020. Accessed Jun. 02, 2020. [Online]. Available: https://github.com/melonproject/oyente

[37] T. Kaiser, 'ChainSecurity's Chaincode Scanner: A Powerful Security Checker for Hyperledger Fabric Smart . . . ', *Medium*, Jun. 15, 2018. https://medium.com/chainsecurity/release-of-hyperchecker-2dff2ebe30cc (Accessed Jun. 03, 2020).

[38] 'CWE – Common Weakness Enumeration'. https://cwe.mitre.org/index.html (Accessed Mar. 20, 2020).

[39] 'SWC – Smart Contract Weakness Classification and Test Cases', *SWC – Smart Contract Weakness Classification and Test Cases*. http://swcregistry.io/ (Accessed Mar. 20, 2020).

[40] L. Luu, D.-H. Chu, H. Olickel, P. Saxena, and A. Hobor, 'Making Smart Contracts Smarter', in *Proceedings of the 2016 ACM SIGSAC Conference on Computer and Communications Security*, Vienna, Austria, Oct. 2016, 254–269. doi: 10.1145/2976749.2978309.

[41] T. Chen, X. Li, X. Luo, and X. Zhang, 'Under-Optimized Smart Contracts Devour your Money', in *2017 IEEE 24th International Conference on Software Analysis, Evolution and Reengineering (SANER)*, Feb. 2017, 442–446. doi: 10.1109/SANER.2017.7884650.

[42] M. Pustišek, J. Turk, and A. Kos, 'Secure Modular Smart Contract Platform for Multi-Tenant 5G Applications', *IEEE Access*, 8, 150626–150646, 2020, doi: 10.1109/ACCESS.2020.3013402.

[43] N. Zahed Benisi, M. Aminian, and B. Javadi, 'Blockchain-Based Decentralized Storage Networks: A Survey', *Journal of Network and Computer Applications*, 162, 102656, Jul 2020, doi: 10.1016/j.jnca.2020.102656.

[44] H. Albreiki, M. Habib Ur Rehman, K. Salah, and D. Svetinovic, 'Trustworthy Blockchain Oracles: Review, Comparison, and Open Research Challenges', *IEEE Access*, 1–1, Jan 2020, doi: 10.1109/ACCESS.2020.2992698.

[45] W. Zheng, Z. Zheng, X. Chen, K. Dai, P. Li, and R. Chen, 'NutBaaS: A Blockchain-as-a-Service Platform', *IEEE Access*, 7, 134422–134433, 2019, doi: 10.1109/ACCESS.2019.2941905.

[46] A. Banafa, 'IoT and Blockchain Convergence: Benefits and Challenges – IEEE Internet of Things', Jan. 10, 2017. http://iot.ieee.org/newsletter/january-2017/iot-and-blockchain-convergence-benefits-and-challenges.html (Accessed Sep. 16, 2020).

[47] M. S. Ali, M. Vecchio, M. Pincheira, K. Dolui, F. Antonelli, and M. H. Rehmani, 'Applications of Blockchains in the Internet of Things: A Comprehensive Survey', *IEEE Communications Surveys Tutorials*, 21, 2, 1676–1717, 2019, doi: 10.1109/COMST.2018.2886932.

[48] J. Bernal Bernabe, J. L. Canovas, J. L. Hernandez-Ramos, R. Torres Moreno, and A. Skarmeta, 'Privacy-Preserving Solutions for Blockchain: Review and Challenges', *IEEE Access*, 7, 164908–164940, 2019, doi: 10.1109/ACCESS.2019.2950872.

[49] L. Hang and D.-H. Kim, 'Design and Implementation of an Integrated IoT Blockchain Platform for Sensing Data Integrity', *Sensors*, 19, 10, Art. no. 10, Jan 2019, doi: 10.3390/s19102228.

[50] 'Self-Sovereign Identity & IoT', Sovrin Foundation, Whitepaper, Aug. 2020. [Online]. Available: https://sovrin.org/wp-content/uploads/SSI-and-IoT-whitepaper.pdf

[51] S. Ding, J. Cao, C. Li, K. Fan, and H. Li, 'A Novel Attribute-Based Access Control Scheme Using Blockchain for IoT', *IEEE Access*, 7, 38431–38441, 2019, doi: 10.1109/ACCESS.2019.2905846.

[52] A. Ouaddah, H. Mousannif, A. Abou Elkalam, and A. Ait Ouahman, 'Access control in the Internet of Things: Big challenges and new opportunities’, *Computer Networks*, 112, 237–262, Jan 2017, doi: 10.1016/j.comnet.2016.11.007.

[53] D. Hardt <dick.hardt@gmail.com>, 'The OAuth 2.0 Authorization Framework'. https://tools.ietf.org/html/rfc6749 (Accessed Apr. 06, 2021).

[54] S. Cirani, M. Picone, P. Gonizzi, L. Veltri, and G. Ferrari, 'IoT-OAS: An OAuth-Based Authorization Service Architecture for Secure Services in IoT Scenarios', *IEEE Sensors Journal*, 15, 2, 1224–1234, Feb 2015, doi: 10.1109/JSEN.2014.2361406.

[55] A. Ouaddah, A. A. Elkalam, and A. A. Ouahman, 'FairAccess: A New Blockchain-Based Access Control Framework for the Internet of Things', *Security and Communication Networks*, 9, 18, 5943–5964, 2016, doi: https://doi.org/10.1002/sec.1748.

[56] S. Patel, A. Sahoo, B. K. Mohanta, S. S. Panda, and D. Jena, 'DAuth: A Decentralized Web Authentication System using Ethereum based Blockchain', in *2019 International Conference on Vision Towards Emerging Trends in Communication and Networking (ViTECoN)*, Mar. 2019, 1–5. doi: 10.1109/ViTECoN.2019.8899393.

[57] S. Hong and H. Kim, 'VaultPoint: A Blockchain-Based SSI Model that Complies with OAuth 2.0', *Electronics*, 9, 8, Art. no. 8, Aug 2020, doi: 10.3390/electronics9081231.

[58] M. Westerlund, S. Leminen, and M. Rajahonka, 'Designing Business Models for the Internet of Things', *Technology Innovation Management Review*, 4, 7, 5–14, 2014.

[59] W. Dors, 'Report on the results of the Industrie 4.0 Platform', Bitkom e.V., Jan. 2016. [Online]. Available: https://www.zvei.org/fileadmin/user_upload/Presse_und_Medien/Publikationen/2016/januar/Implementation_Strategy_Industrie_4.0_-_Report_on_the_results_of_Industrie_4.0_Platform/Implementation-Strategy-Industrie-40-ENG.pdf

[60] G. Jain, and M. Pai, 'Talking Cars: A Survey of Protocols for Connected Vehicle Communication', *Wipro Digital*, Jun. 20, 2018. https://wiprodigital.com/2018/06/20/talking-cars-a-survey-of-protocols-for-connected-vehicle-communication/ (Accessed Jun. 07, 2021).

[61] X. Yao, 'Evolving Artificial Neural Networks', *Proceedings of the IEEE*, 87, 9, 1423–1447, Sep 1999, doi: 10.1109/5.784219.

[62] J. Carter, K. Schmid, K. Waters, L. Betzhold, R. Mataosky, and J. Halleran, 'Lidar 101: An Introduction to Lidar Technology, Data, and Applications', NOAA Coastal Services Center, Charleston, Nov. 2012. [Online]. Available: https://coast.noaa.gov/data/digitalcoast/pdf/lidar-101.pdf

[63] N. Živić, 'Distributed Ledger Technology for Automotive Production 4.0', in *2020 28th Telecommunications Forum (ᵀᴱᴸFOR)*, Nov. 2020, 1–3. doi: 10.1109/ᵀᴱᴸFOR51502.2020.9306594.

[64] N. Živić, 'Distributed Ledger Technologies for Car Industry 4.0', in *Proceedings of the 2020 International Conference on Computer Communication and Information Systems*, Ho Chi Minh City Viet Nam, Aug. 2020, 45–51. doi: 10.1145/3418994.3418998.

[65] A. E. Saddik, 'Digital Twins: The Convergence of Multimedia Technologies', *IEEE MultiMedia*, 25, 2, 87–92, Apr 2018, doi: 10.1109/MMUL.2018.023121167.

[66] Daimler, 'Production is Becoming Smart. Industry 4.0 and the Networked Factory', *Daimler*. https://www.daimler.com/innovation/case/connectivity/industry-4-0.html (Accessed Jun. 07, 2021).

[67] 'Circulor Offers Transparency for Mineral Sourcing with Oracle Blockchain Platform'. https://www.oracle.com/customers/circulor-1-blockchain/ (Accessed Jun. 07, 2021).

[68] I. Afanasyev, A. Kolotov, R. Rezin, K. Danilov, A. Kashevnik, and V. Jotsov, 'Blockchain Solutions for Multi-Agent Robotic Systems: Related Work and Open Questions', in *Proceedings of the 24th Conference of Open Innovations Association FRUCT*, Helsinki, Uusimaa, FIN, Apr. 2019, 551–555.

[69] N. Teslya and I. Ryabchikov, 'Blockchain-based Platform Architecture for Industrial IoT', in *21st Conference of Open Innovations Association (FRUCT)*, Nov. 2017, 321–329. doi: 10.23919/FRUCT.2017.8250199.

[70] A. Kapitonov, I. Berman, S. Lonshakov, and A. Krupenkin, 'Blockchain Based Protocol for Economical Communication in Industry 4.0', in *Crypto Valley Conference on Blockchain Technology (CVCBT)*, Jun. 2018, 41–44. doi: 10.1109/CVCBT.2018.00010.

[71] A. Kapitonov, S. Lonshakov, A. Krupenkin, and I. Berman, 'Blockchain-Based Protocol of Autonomous Business Activity for Multi-Agent Systems Consisting of UAVs', in *Workshop on*

Research, Education and Development of Unmanned Aerial Systems (RED-UAS), Oct. 2017, 84–89. doi: 10.1109/RED-UAS.2017.8101648.

[72] A. Sharma, *et al*, 'Communication and Networking Technologies for UAVs: A Survey', *Journal of Network and Computer Applications*, 168, 102739, Oct 2020, doi: 10.1016/j.jnca.2020. 102739.

[73] N. Teslya and A. Smirnov, 'Blockchain-based Framework for Ontology-Oriented Robots' Coalition Formation in Cyberphysical Systems&#x2019, in *MATEC Web of Conferences*, 2018, vol. 161, 03018. doi: 10.1051/matecconf/201816103018.

[74] V. Lopes, L. A. Alexandre, and N. Pereira, 'Controlling Robots using Artificial Intelligence and a Consortium Blockchain', *arXiv:1903.00660 [cs]*, Mar. 2019, Accessed Jun. 07, 2021. [Online]. Available: http://arxiv.org/abs/1903.00660

[75] E. Castello, O. Rudovic, T. Hardjono, and A. Pentland, 'RoboChain: A Secure Data-Sharing Framework for Human-Robot Interaction', presented at the The Tenth International Conference on eHealth, Telemedicine, and Social Medicine eTELEMED, Feb. 2018. [Online]. Available: https://www.researchgate.net/publication/323164908_RoboChain_A_Secure_Data-Sharing_Framework_for_Human-Robot_Interaction

[76] N. Cvar, J. Trilar, A. Kos, M. Volk, and E. Stojmenova Duh, 'The Use of IoT Technology in Smart Cities and Smart Villages: Similarities, Differences, and Future Prospects', *Sensors*, 20, 14, Art. no. 14, Jan 2020, doi: 10.3390/s20143897.

[77] C. Greer *et al.*, 'NIST Framework and Roadmap for Smart Grid Interoperability Standards, Release 3.0', National Institute of Standards and Technology, NIST SP 1108r3, Oct. 2014. Accessed Jan. 25, 2018. [Online]. Available: http://nvlpubs.nist.gov/nistpubs/SpecialPublications/NIST.SP.1108r3.pdf

[78] M. Pustišek, N. Bremond, and A. Kos, 'Electric Switch with Ethereum Blockchain Support', *IPSI TIR*, 14, 1, 21–28, Jan 2018.

Index

https://doi.org/10.1515/9783110681130-006